Brazilian Jiu-Jitsu

Self-Defense

TECHNIQUES

Brazilian Jiu-Jitsu
Self-Defense
TECHNIQUES

Royce Gracie and
Charles Gracie

with Kid Peligro

Position photographs by Tom Page

INVISIBLE CITIES PRESS

MONTPELIER, VERMONT

Invisible Cities Press
50 State Street
Montpelier, VT 05602
www.invisiblecitiespress.com

The Library of Congress has catalogued this book as follows

Gracie, Royce.
Brazilian jiu-jitsu self-defense techniques /
Royce Gracie and Charles Gracie with Kid Peligro.
p. cm.
ISBN 1-931229-27-9 (paper)
1. Jiu-jitsu—Brazil. I. Gracie, Charles. II. Peligro, Kid. III. Title.

GV1114 .G75 2002
796.815—dc21
2002027339

Anyone practicing the techniques in this book does so at his or her own risk. The authors and the publisher assume no responsibility for the use or misuse of information contained in this book or for any injuries that may occur as a result of practicing the techniques contained herein. The illustrations and text are for informational purposes only. It is imperative to practice these holds and techniques under the strict supervision of a qualified instructor. Additionally, one should consult a physician before embarking on any demanding physical activity.

Printed in Canada

Book design by Peter Holm, Sterling Hill Productions
with layout assistance from Terri Klein

FIRST EDITION

This book is dedicated to the many members of the Gracie family for their tireless efforts and sacrifice over the past seven decades to spread the word about Brazilian jiu-jitsu throughout the world. It is also dedicated to our immediate families and loved ones for their love, support, and friendship. Finally, it is dedicated to all people who choose to learn self-defense and to protect themselves and their loved ones.

Contents

Introduction

*C*ongratulations! By buying this book, you have just made a commitment to learning the safest and most effective system of self-defense available. *Brazilian Jiu-Jitsu Self-Defense Techniques* will teach you how to neutralize any attacker in almost any situation without causing serious injury. It will give you a confidence on the streets you may never have had.

If you are at all familiar with Brazilian jiu-jitsu, you probably know that it has revolutionized the martial arts world in the past decade, and you probably know that Gracie is perhaps the best-known name in the martial arts. What you may not know is that the Gracies began teaching Brazilian jiu-jitsu as a means of self-defense, beginning in Rio de Janeiro in the 1920s. As Brazilian jiu-jitsu has come to dominate mixed martial arts (MMA) competitions, and emphasis has shifted to the sport aspect of Brazilian jiu-jitsu, the streetworthiness of the art has been neglected. On the streets, fancy competition sweeps and gi lapel chokes are not effective. Therefore, in a sense this book takes Brazilian jiu-jitsu back to its roots by taking it out of the ring.

As Royce Gracie explains, "A fight does not start with a referee asking if you are ready. It generally starts with an aggressive action, an unexpected attack. If you can't escape from that attack and bring the situation to your comfort zone, then you are in for a long day. I have seen many people well versed in Brazilian jiu-jitsu get into trouble because they couldn't escape from a certain hold."

What is it about Brazilian jiu-jitsu that makes it so effective as a self-defense system? We can break the answer into four main points: it is designed to work even when you are surprised and in a poor position, it is designed by small people to defeat larger ones, it allows you to develop instantaneous reactions by practicing in extremely lifelike exercises, and it provides you with a range of severity in dealing with your attacker. Let's examine these points one by one.

1. Surprise

To understand Brazilian jiu-jitsu, you must understand the difference between a *grappling* art and a *striking* art. Grappling arts (such as jiu-jitsu and judo) use wrestling-like holds to control an opponent, while striking arts (such as karate) use kicks and punches to incapacitate an opponent. Striking arts work best when you know an opponent is there and can launch an attack before he is close. Grappling arts are designed for close contact, so even if you've been attacked from behind or are caught in a clinch—even a headlock—you will have a range of effective responses at your disposal. Brazilian jiu-jitsu famously turned the martial arts world upside-down by showing that, when flat on his back with his opponent on top of him, a skilled Brazilian jiu-jitsu practitioner was still in an extremely favorable position. Having an instant and effective reaction to an attack makes all the difference in the outcome, and the Brazilian jiu-jitsu self-defense system places much emphasis on this element of surprise, as we will see in the positions.

2. Size and Strength

A karate chop is not always the answer. As Royce points out, "It is very important to realize that striking someone bigger and tougher than you may just aggravate the situation. Take, for example, a small person trying to punch a 260-pound man; it is just going to make him angry. With our techniques, we use the pain from an arm lock or another submission hold to control the situation." Because Brazilian jiu-jitsu was developed by men of relatively small build, it had to develop ways to defeat larger opponents that could be employed by smaller ones. This makes it the ideal self-defense system. It takes little strength—just skill—to properly execute a guillotine choke, wrist lock, or arm bar that will have your attacker begging for mercy and completely in your control.

3. Lifelike Training

A further drawback to the striking arts is that, when training against a live partner, at some level you have to "pull your punches." Because the striking arts are designed to injure an opponent with kicks or strikes, you can only go so far while sparring before risking injury. You never get the feel of how quickly things happen in a real fight, or what it is like to actually punch someone. But, because Brazilian jiu-jitsu has little use for kicks and punches—instead relying on chokes, arm locks, and other submission holds—it can be practiced exactly the same way it would go down in an actual fight. This may not seem significant at first, but in the precious seconds of a real street fight it can make all the difference. Royce and Charles have seen skilled martial artists who turned out to be hothouse flowers under the pressure of a real fight; when faced with no-rules situations that didn't follow the carefully prescribed rules of their training, they wilted. In contrast, a Brazilian jiu-jitsu practitioner, by sparring again and again under lifelike conditions, develops automatic responses to a full variety of attacks. Virtually no thought is required. Like hitting a baseball or surfing a wave, it becomes muscle memory. Only then is it truly useful in an unexpected situation.

4. Severity

When asked about what differentiates Brazilian jiu-jitsu self-defense from other types of self-defense, Royce and Charles are quick to reply. "In our style, the techniques allow you to choose the severity level of the response. If the person you are facing is a friend who is temporarily out of his senses, you can control him without hurting him. However, if you are dealing with a criminal or a deliberate act to injure you or a loved one, you can apply a more suitable response level and cause as much damage as you need to." Because Brazilian jiu-jitsu emphasizes control, not striking, it is particularly sought out by people whose job it is to subdue individuals without hurting them—bar bouncers, policemen, security personnel. It is a great self-defense option to have for anyone else as well—far better than being forced to injure someone so seriously with kicks and strikes that they can no longer attack you. Of course, if an attacker is so dangerous that you need to put him out of commission—so you can get away, for instance—then it is a simple matter to follow through and break the wrist, elbow, or shoulder joint that you have in a lock.

There, in a nutshell, are some of the reasons why Brazilian jiu-jitsu self-defense is the perfect system for most people who want to learn to protect themselves. We'll explore some of these same issues in further detail in the training chapter. But where, you may ask, did Brazilian jiu-jitsu come from? Why was it able to revolutionize the martial arts? What makes it so unique? To understand the answers to these questions, first you need to learn a little history.

The History of Brazilian Jiu-Jitsu

In 1801 a Scottish immigrant by the name of George Gracie moved to the state of Pará in northeastern Brazil. There he and his family lived for many years. In the early 1900s a Japanese man named Mitsuyo Maeda moved to the same area. The Japanese government was eager to form a colony in Brazil, and Maeda was there to help the colony prosper. In addition to his political skills, Maeda happened to be a former champion in the Japanese art of jiu-jitsu, and he began teaching lessons in Brazil, hoping to pass on the tradition. He became close friends with Gastão Gracie, the grandson of George Gracie. Gastao was involved in politics and used his influence to help Maeda and the Japanese colony. Maeda, in return, taught Gastão's son Carlos the art of jiu-jitsu.

In 1925, after moving to Rio de Janeiro, Carlos and his brothers opened the first Academy of Gracie Jiu-Jitsu, in the Flamengo area of the city. At the time, Rio de Janeiro was the capital of Brazil. The academy quickly became an enormous success, and soon the brothers were teaching the top politicians and personalities of the country.

The Gracie Academy had many instructors teaching classes all day long. What they taught, at first, was the traditional Japanese style of jiu-jitsu Carlos had learned from Maeda. Like judo, it was a grappling style of combat with many formal rules. Weighted down under centuries of ritualized tradition and technique, there was little room for innovation. But, half a world away from Japan's influence, the sport found room to breathe in Brazil. Carlos and his brothers knew little of formal martial arts and were thus able to simply discover what works best in any given situation. Because the Gracies were free to emphasize what was effective and leave behind anything that didn't serve a purpose, the sport quickly evolved from its parent sport into something quite different and came to be known as Gracie jiu-jitsu.

Highly influential in the development of Gracie jiu-jitsu was Helio Gracie, Carlos's younger brother. All the Gracies were slight of frame, but Helio was particularly small and frail. He even suffered from spells of dizziness that prevented him from attending school. Young Helio would spend his days watching the others teach all day long. He observed more closely than anyone realized, because one day when Carlos was unable to make it to a private class, Helio offered to teach the student. Helio was sixteen years old and weighed 140 pounds, and the student was skeptical but agreed. At the end of the lesson the student was so impressed with Helio's teaching style that he asked

Carlos if Helio could be his teacher. From that day on Helio Gracie became a full instructor at the academy.

Over the next few years, Carlos and Helio developed their new style. Because of his small stature and frailty, Helio could not use many of the Japanese moves that were based on power and speed, so he developed new leverages and new ways of doing moves. As Helio tells it, "My brother Carlos was very athletic, quick, and flexible. He could do those moves easily, but myself, I was a sickly young kid and couldn't use the same leverage points or the same speed, so I had to adapt." With Helio doing more of the instructional work, Carlos was able to dedicate himself to the managerial side of the family business and to developing the famed "Gracie Diet." (A diet based on food groups and how they combine with each other, it has been perfected and used by the family for the past seventy-five years.)

Helio turned out to be a brilliant innovator, and the style he developed proved to be victorious against all others, regardless of size. Helio Gracie became the top sports figure in Brazil in the 1930s. Fighting in public events in front of tens of thousands of spectators, his reputation grew immensely. For over two decades the Gracies accepted many challenges and fought a variety of opponents from different backgrounds and of different sizes. In one extreme example, brother Osvaldo Gracie, who weighed 140 pounds, fought John Baldy, who tipped the scales at 360 pounds. Osvaldo defeated Baldy with a choke hold in just two minutes.

Eventually the Gracies' fame reached outside the borders of their homeland, back to Japan, home of the most skilled martial artists in the world at that time. The Gracie brothers issued a challenge to the best martial artist Japan had ever produced, Masahiko Kimura. Kimura stipulated that he would not fight Helio until Helio proved himself against the second-ranked fighter in the world at that time, known as Kato.

Kato was forty pounds heavier than Helio and considered by many to be the best jiu-jitsu technician in the world. The two fought a legendary battle to a draw. In the rematch, Helio choked Kato unconscious with his favorite move, the front lapel choke.

Master Kimura then challenged Helio to a fight. Kimura stated at the time that if anyone so slight could survive three minutes in the ring with him, he would consider it a defeat. Helio, despite the huge weight difference and strength difference, battled valiantly for thirteen minutes before he was caught in a brilliant arm lock called "the Kimura"—now a standard move in Brazilian jiu-jitsu. Seeing his brother's arm about to be broken, Carlos threw in the towel.

For the next seventy-five years the Gracie family dedicated itself to the preservation and dissemination of this great fighting style—once called Gracie jiu-jitsu, now more widely known as Brazilian jiu-jitsu. In the past ten years, the newest generation of Gracies have brought a popularity to the sport beyond the wildest dreams of Carlos and Helio. It is time to meet two of the most dynamic members of the family, Royce and Charles, along with their good friend Kid Peligro.

Meet the Authors

Royce

November 12, 1993: a new pay-per-view event makes its debut in America—the Ultimate Fighting Championship. The concept was simple: pit eight experts in different martial arts against each other in single-elimination fights, with no rules and no time limits, to learn once and for all which martial art is most effective in real-life situations. Among the contestants was a 380-pound sumo wrestler, a 215-pound world champion kickboxer, a pancrase champion, and a skinny, 175-pound man dressed in a white kimono. Over the two hours of the event, that skinny man defeated every opponent without so much as throwing a single punch on his way to the title and the sudden attention of the entire martial arts community. His name? Royce Gracie.

That night, Royce Gracie became one of the most recognized names in martial arts and launched the Brazilian jiu-jitsu revolution around the world. Far from being an overnight sensation, this was something Royce had been preparing for his entire life.

The second-youngest son of the legendary Grandmaster Helio Gracie, Royce grew up in Rio de Janeiro, Brazil, in a family of fighters. Young Royce spent his childhood watching the masters of the sport teaching: his father, Helio, brothers Rorion and Rickson, and cousin Rolls were the head instructors at the Gracie Academy at this time. Royce began absorbing their teachings and learning all the details and techniques exchanged between family members.

Royce began competing in tournaments at age eight. He received his blue belt at age sixteen and was promoted to black belt in less than two years. At the age of seventeen, by invitation of his brother Rorion, Royce moved to the United States to help popularize Brazilian jiu-jitsu. Arriving in America without speaking a word of English, Royce immediately went to work teaching. Running classes out of their garage, Royce and Rorion taught for hours on end. Their school grew by word of mouth, and in 1991 Rorion and Royce opened the Gracie Jiu-Jitsu Academy in Torrance, California. Today it is one of the largest martial arts schools in the country.

In 1993, Royce got the chance to fulfill his family's lifelong dream of showing America and the world the style his family had pioneered. The Ultimate Fighting Championship debuted in Denver, Colorado. Instead of a regular boxing ring, the arena was an octagon made of chain-link fence to keep the fighters from escaping through the ropes.

Royce was selected to be the Gracie representative at the Ultimate Fighting Championship by his father and brothers despite the fact that he had never fought in a single professional fight. Royce was not a total fight novice, however; he had plenty of experience defending the family name in informal challenges. Years before, the family had issued the famed "Gracie Challenge," in which they offered $100,000 to anyone who could defeat one of the brothers in a no-rules match. Needless to say, the challenge attracted many takers, but no winners.

The UFC was broadcast to the largest pay-per-view audience ever to that date. When the time came for Royce to face his first opponent in the UFC, boxer Art Jimmerson, the world was introduced to the Gracie family and its style. The family marched into the arena in single file, with one of the brothers leading the way for the entourage and Royce in second position. It was the birth of "The Gracie Train," a show of unity from a family dedicated to their art for decades. As the fight started, Royce rapidly clinched Jimmerson, took him down, and mounted him. The boxer, not used to fighting with his back against the ground, quickly gave up.

Royce's next opponent was Ken Shamrock. Shamrock had a huge name in Japan, having won the prestigious King of Pancrase title in the Japanese professional fight circuit. A very experienced fighter, with solid ground-fighting skills, Shamrock outweighed Royce by thirty pounds. As the fight started, again Royce clinched and took the fight to the ground. Unlike his predecessor, Shamrock did not panic or give up, and the two fighters exchanged position until Royce's greater skill allowed him to secure a choke, ending the fight.

Royce's opponent in the final round was the kickboxer Gerard Gordeau. Gordeau was a menacing figure, standing at 6'5" and 215 pounds, with long legs for powerful kicks. It appeared to be a mismatch against the lanky Gracie, but the match followed the same script: Royce clinched, took Gordeau to the ground, and proceeded to choke him into submission. Using his family's techniques, Royce Gracie defeated three opponents in one night, and in the process blew the minds of traditional martial artists. No one could comprehend what had happened, but everyone wanted to learn more about the young man and his combat style. Royce went on to win two additional UFC titles and is still the only man in the history of no-holds-barred matches to defeat four opponents in a single night.

After its success in the Ultimate Fighting Championships, the Gracie Academy became the Mecca for Brazilian jiu-jitsu, quadrupling in size in just two months. With hordes of eager students knocking at his door, Royce immersed himself in his teaching, hoping to expand the reach of Brazilian jiu-jitsu to the greatest number of people. For five years Royce spent most of his days refining his craft and his teaching methods. But eventually, the draw of the ring was too much and the most recognized person in jiu-jitsu was lured back to fight, this time in Japan. The event was Pride, the largest MMA show in Japan and perhaps the world.

Royce's first match was against a Japanese Idol, Nobuhiko Takada, one of the most famous pro wrestlers in Japan. Royce punished Takada the entire first fifteen-minute round and Takada declined to return for the next. The win set up a match against Kazushi Sakuraba, considered by many at the time to be the best middleweight fighter in the world. In what became an all-time classic, and the longest professional fight in recent history, Royce and Sakuraba kicked, punched, and exchanged submission attempts for an astounding ninety minutes. Only a broken foot at the end of the sixth fifteen-minute round forced Royce to finally abandon the fight.

Today Royce is privileged to spread the techniques perfected by his father all over the world. He maintains a rigorous travel schedule of seminars and classes, and his list of students is without peer. Royce has taught celebrities such as Chuck Norris, Ed O'Neill, Guy Ritchie, and Nicholas Cage. He has also been very active with the CIA, FBI, DEA, Secret Service, Army Rangers, Army Special Forces, Navy Seals, and many sheriff and police departments.

Royce makes his home in Torrance, California, with his wife, Marianne, and his sons, Khonry, Khor, and Kheydon. He spends his days perfecting his skills and eagerly awaits his next fight.

Charles

All his life Charles Gracie has been trying to stay out of the limelight and work behind the scenes. Charles most values improving his technical skills and his teaching, along with his passionate dedication to his family. This quiet and unassuming Gracie, however, has had the limelight forced upon him and has risen to the occasion.

Born in Rio de Janeiro, Brazil, the oldest son of Robson Gracie (son of Carlos Gracie) and brother to Renzo and Ralph, Charles started early in the family ways, learning Brazilian jiu-jitsu while still a toddler. Soon after, he was under the tutelage of his uncle, the legendary Rolls Gracie.

One of the best fighters in the family and widely recognized as the leader of the Brazilian jiu-jitsu movement at that time, Rolls would pick up Charles at his home, take him to the Rio Branco and Copacabana Schools, and share his wisdom and techniques with his young nephew. Charles came to consider Rolls his second father. In 1981, when Charles was seventeen and had achieved the rank of purple belt, Rolls died tragically in a hang gliding accident. For Charles the loss was devastating.

After Rolls's death, Charles took time away from the sport to recover. The loss of his mentor and close friend left him unmotivated. Soon, however, the family roots took hold. Brazilian jiu-jitsu is in Charles's blood, and with renewed motivation and a desire to continue the legacy of his uncle, Charles rededicated himself to learning the family art. When he returned, Charles trained under Grandmaster Helio Gracie and his uncles Carlos Jr. and Reylson. Charles received his black belt in 1985 at the age of twenty-one.

After receiving his black belt, Charles moved to the state of Bahia, north of Rio de Janeiro, where he lived until 1997. Charles was the driving force in establishing the Brazilian Jiu-Jitsu Federation of Bahia and became one of the leading figures of the sport there, helping organize some of the first competitions in that state. While living in Bahia, Charles met his wife, Tatiana. They have two children, Riury and Victoria.

One of Charles's first detours into the limelight came while he was living in Bahia. When his better-known brothers were unavailable, Charles was asked to participate in a no-rules professional event. He was matched against Assuerio Silva, a 231-pound fighter with previous professional experience. Charles trained for six months for the fight. In front of thousands of screaming fans, Charles, weighing in at 180 pounds, used classic Brazilian jiu-jitsu techniques against his larger opponent. As the fight started, Charles quickly clinched, while avoiding his opponent's powerful punches. He then took Silva down and methodically adjusted his position until he achieved the mounted position. From there Charles administered a barrage of punches, forcing Silva to turn over to protect himself. At two-and-a-half minutes Charles submitted Silva with a choke from the back.

By the late 1990s Charles felt that his mission in Bahia was complete, and he was ready for new horizons and new challenges. He moved to San Francisco in 1998, where he now maintains his academy. During his second year in America, again destiny unexpectedly called Charles to task. While accompanying his team to the California State Titles, he was asked to fill in for an injured fighter in a professional Superfight. Because of the importance of such matches in popularizing the sport, Charles felt the necessity to fight, despite having a knee injury that kept him from training. Charles faced another black belt. The match opened and his adversary scored the first points with a reversal. From then on, satisfied with the lead and the possibility of defeating a Gracie family member, Charles's opponent played conservatively, blocking Charles's attacks while awaiting the end of the match. With less than one minute to go, Charles reached deep into his technical arsenal and, with a relentless flurry of attacks, Charles was able to defeat his opponent with a "triangle" choke.

Charles has spent the past four years concentrating on promoting Brazilian jiu-jitsu in the United States. One of his main desires is to maintain the sport's authenticity. He does this by participating in the organization of tournaments and is currently involved in the organization of the American Federation of Brazilian Jiu-Jitsu. It was Charles's strong desire to spread the family teachings to all that caused him to see the need for a book of self-defense techniques using the Gracie methods. Bringing together his cousin Royce and good friend Kid Peligro to participate in the project made it a dream come true for this tireless devotee of Brazilian jiu-jitsu.

kid

Kid Peligro has been involved in the martial arts for most of his life. He attained the rank of brown belt in American kenpo before discovering Brazilian jiu-jitsu. His passion and dedication to the sport earned him the level of black belt after ten years of practice. Peligro is best known as one of the leading writers in the sport. His two World Titles in the Masters Division are a testament to his knowledge and commitment to the art. Peligro has a reputation of being on the cutting edge of the technical development of the sport. He is responsible for regular columns in two of the largest MMA magazines in the world—*Grappling* and *Gracie Magazine*—as well as the most widely read Internet MMA news page, ADCC News.

Kid Peligro's broad involvement with Brazilian jiu-jitsu and MMA events has led him to travel to the four corners of the earth, covering Brazilian jiu-jitsu, submission grappling, and MMA events in America, Brazil, Japan, and the Middle East. Considered the ambassador of Brazilian jiu-jitsu, Peligro is dedicated to spreading the word of the sport to a wide audience. As a respected personality in the sport, Peligro has been fortunate to have studied, trained and become friends with the best instructors and practitioners in the business. Peligro's journalist background, along with his deep sense of commitment to furthering the spread of Brazilian jiu-jitsu, made him the perfect person to translate the techniques of Royce and Charles Gracie into words. Peligro was also the editor, cocreator, and organizer of Renzo and Royler Gracie's breakthrough book *Brazilian Jiu-Jitsu: Theory and Technique.*

Training Guidelines

*t*his book is structured to replicate, as closely as possible, what it is like to take private classes with a master like Royce or Charles. The sequence of the positions shown here is the order that the Gracie family has determined, over seventy-five years, is the best for students to learn. Royce and Charles went to great efforts to make sure the sequence is the best possible way to transmit the techniques to the reader. In each technique, the commands in *red italics* are Royce's and Charles's verbal commands. These are the same commands that they use in their private self-defense lessons. Royce is famous for not wasting time with unnecessary words in his lessons, and the italicized commands mimic his style. *Do this, do this, do that,* they say. By following them, you will receive the essence of Brazilian jiu-jitsu self-defense in a very concentrated form. After the commands, more in-depth explanations, with important details of the moves, are offered.

How often should you train? Both Royce and Charles Gracie recommend that a student practice the moves for a *minimum* of a half hour once a week. A much better training regimen is to practice three to four times a week for at least one hour. Not everyone's lifestyle can support this, and if you can only practice once a week for a half hour, you will still get some benefit from the training. A typical student training with the masters will attend three to four lessons a week. At the academy the student will usually be exposed to three to five techniques a day, depending on the complexity of the moves, during the first 60 minutes of the lesson.

A typical class starts with stretching exercises followed by a warm-up session in which the student prepares his body for the training. The stretching should concentrate especially on the legs (toe-touches) and hip area (forward and side bends, circling the hips very slowly clockwise and counterclockwise) to assure the maximum range of motion and to avoid injuries such as pulled muscles, while the warm-up exercises will concentrate on making sure all the body joints are loose and ready to perform.

A common warm-up routine involves circling the arms, forward and backward, slowly at first, then gradually increasing speed to assure full mobility. The same routine is applied to the hips, knees, and ankles. Following that, concentrate on the neck muscles, since both tournament competitions and street fights generally involve some sort of attack to that area. Again, circling motions and side-to-side action will ensure that the neck is properly prepared.

Another area of great importance to properly stretch is the back.

Deep bends and side-to-side stretches are recommended. Back warm-up exercises consisting of bridging (lifting your hips up by pushing off your legs and balancing on the back of your head, while laying with your back on the ground), circling the upper body through its full range of motion, or simply lifting the hips off the ground while laying on your back for at least 10 repetitions, will suffice. The stretching and warm-up period varies with each person but should take at least 10 to 15 minutes.

Once a technique is shown, the student does repetitions slowly, with a willing partner who does not resist, until he begins to comprehend the mechanics and the leverages that are involved in that particular technique. It is extremely important for a student to practice the techniques correctly at slow speed. Do not rush through the moves and sacrifice correctness in the process.

Muscle memory only develops from repetition. If one never practices a move, it will not come out correctly under duress. As Royce puts it: "Speed is a consequence of repetition! The tenth time you do the move, you will do it better than the first time. After a hundred times, you should start feeling very comfortable. If you are still having problems after a thousand repetitions, then we have a problem!" Especially in self-defense situations—where a person must decide, quickly, which move to use and how—you can't afford to waste precious seconds thinking. Therefore, we recommend that you diligently practice these moves until they become automatic. Only then will you be able to have confidence in what you have learned. And that confidence can go a long way. Sometimes, in fact, you may be able to defuse confrontation before it occurs, simply because of the calm and confident way that you conduct yourself. And even if you are attacked, most attackers aren't expecting their victims to have ready responses at hand, so the element of surprise you gain from an instantaneous response will put almost all attackers on the defensive immediately.

Most of the defenses in this book are demonstrated against right-handed attackers, since that is what you are most likely to encounter. However, you don't want to be at a loss if attacked by a southpaw, so practice some of these positions (particularly the weapons attacks) with the lefts and rights reversed. Eventually, you should be equally comfortable using either hand and foot.

Another important thing to keep in mind when training is to try to simulate, as much as possible, a real-life attack. At first you must master the techniques by executing them at slow speed under very controlled conditions, but as you progress and become more and more adept, you need your partner to begin to resist. Eventually your partner should try to be as "real" as possible, throwing punches that are nearly real, swinging the bat like an attacker would swing the bat, and attempting real headlocks, chokes, bear hugs, and so on. As you get proficient, your partner should begin to attempt to anticipate your moves and counter them. Brazilian jiu-jitsu was able to evolve into a martial art that usually defeats other martial arts by letting new moves arise out of the free give-and-take between two opponents. Having a partner who can force you to think on your feet and never get stale is the true key to becoming a top martial artist.

The Importance of the Basics

Before we get into the positions themselves, there are two basic techniques that are essential to correctly learning the rest. They are emphasized here because a beginning student might be tempted to ignore them and move on to the more "exciting" positions. That would be a grave mistake, as it is impossible to be a truly successful Brazilian jiu-jitsu martial artist without having a deep familiarity with these techniques.

Base

In this book we constantly refer to staying in base or dropping in base. This means dropping your hips and spreading your feet so that your center of gravity is low and you have a firm base of support—essential to defeating a larger, stronger opponent. Because Brazilian jiu-jitsu is based on leverage and position, it is no exaggeration to say that your success depends on learning to quickly get into proper base. That is why the proper ways to stay, and get, in base are the first two techniques in the book.

One of the tricks to maintaining your base is to imagine a string tied to your waist, pulling you down to the ground. Keeping that thought in mind will greatly help you to stay in base. Additionally, staying in base involves placement of your hips. The hips connect the upper body to the lower body, and they are the key to achieving and maintaining proper base. For best understanding of the concept you should closely examine the pictures, read the text, and then practice the positions. You will be able to "feel" when you are in good base.

Falling and Rolling

The other key series of techniques you must master is properly falling down and properly rolling. Because of their importance, these techniques are also shown in the first few lessons. Given that in any fight situation there is a strong possibility that you will end up on the ground, you cannot feel safe in a street fight if you don't know how to properly fall. To become a fearless and unhesitant Brazilian jiu-jitsu practitioner, you must make the ground your friend. You are not afraid to hit it, you are not afraid to be on it. This will put you at a serious advantage over most adversaries.

Again, there are some special points that should be brought up about proper falling techniques. Always attempt to keep your head up and away from hitting the ground. You don't want to hit your head and become stunned or lose consciousness. You should also not be stiff; let your body relax as it touches the ground. Additionally, you can take away the impact of the fall by hitting the ground with your extended lower arm first.

The Element of Surprise

The importance of having an instantaneous reaction to an attack has already been touched on, but this is such a vital component of the Brazilian jiu-jitsu self-defense system that it is worth repeating. Practice, practice, practice. Once your reactions to possible attacks become automatic, without having to waste time thinking about what the attack is and what defense should be employed, you will greatly increase the efficiency of these techniques. Few victims have instantaneous responses at their disposal, and this element of surprise will put most attackers on the run—if they are still able to, that is.

No Substitute for a Qualified Instructor

Although this book is designed to be the next best thing to Royce's and Charles's personal classes, it obviously isn't the same thing. No book could be. An instructor can watch what you do and give you feedback moment by moment. An instructor can make you feel the moves and can personalize training to your individual strengths and weaknesses. He can answer questions. You probably cannot become a self-defense expert from book-learning alone.

Having said that, however, we must emphasize that this book is still invaluable to any self-defense student. It can serve students in two distinct ways. For those who do not have an instructor, it can serve as a guideline for correctness. You can learn the positions and undoubtedly make yourself better prepared to handle any unexpected aggression. Then, when you do have a chance to train with an instructor, you will have a great base to build on.

For those who have qualified instruction, this book can be an essential reference guide. Everything seems clear in the classes, but then you try to repeat them at home and end up asking yourself, "Wait, what am I supposed to do next?" Being able to view the positions at home when you're practicing makes all the difference, and you will find yourself referring to this book again and again.

A Last Word

Yes, learning the self-defense techniques in this book will make you safer in the world. But the benefits of learning a martial art like Brazilian jiu-jitsu go well beyond that. As Charles and Royce say, "The importance of Brazilian jiu-jitsu is that all the challenges you face in training will help you achieve a high level of confidence and self-esteem. Not only does training increase your coordination, but knowing you have such control over your body (and any physical situations that may arise) also improves your emotional control. All that will make you a better businessperson, a better worker, a better student, a better brother or sister, a better parent. Jiu-jitsu helps you learn that you can solve any situation you face. In learning self-defense and jiu-jitsu, you realize that you are capable of escaping from extremely adverse situations. And that experience translates into everyday life."

Dropping in base

The ability to stay on your feet is very important in a street situation. Once knocked down, it becomes more difficult to defend yourself. Therefore, a solid base is a must.

1 Royce stands in a natural posture. He is relaxed, feet spread shoulder-width, hands on his sides, and torso centered. From this stance, Royce can quickly react to any attack.

2 ***Drop down: feet apart, head forward, and butt down.*** Royce now drops in base. He opens both feet out at the same time to widen his base, leans forward with his torso, and lowers his hips. He closes his elbows by his hips and tightens his hands into fists. His base is now spread out, but his body remains centered in relation to his feet.

3 This is the side view of the correct posture. Notice how Royce's hips are slightly back from his feet to compensate for the weight of his head and body leaning forward. His elbows are close to his waist and his arms are tight. Royce's legs are bent so that he can quickly adjust to any changes by his opponent. It is important to drop straight down in base, as if you are doing a set of jumping jacks, instead of stepping out to the side. By properly dropping in base, you will maintain your balance the entire time. If you step out while being attacked you run the risk of losing your balance.

Maintaining your base

A key to any self-defense situation is the ability to maintain your base of support. If a person can push or pull you off-balance, you lose control of the situation. Therefore it is essential for practicing the techniques in this book that you learn to keep your balance at all times.

1 Royce pulls on Charles. *Lean back and put your weight on your back leg, back straight, hips slightly forward, head straight.* By keeping his weight on his back leg, with his hips forward and his head straight, Charles can counter Royce's pulling action. It is important for Charles not to commit too much weight to his back leg, or he will fall back if Royce decides to let go. Think of how your body acts when you are pulling on a rope. This situation requires a similar posture.

2 Do this exercise with a partner to get a feel for the constant subtle shifts in balance needed.

3 Royce pushes Charles. *Push with your back leg, hips forward, weight on your front leg, head straight.* Again, Charles shifts his weight to counteract the action, in this case pushing forward and shifting his weight to his front leg, keeping his head straight and hips forward without overcommitting to either leg.

Single-handed wrist grab (thumb up)

A very common situation in any confrontation is for an attacker to grab your wrist and pull. This can be especially difficult to escape if the aggressor is quite strong.

1 Charles grabs Royce's right wrist with his left hand.

2 *Maintain your base and turn your wrist up toward the thumb.* By going in the direction of the thumb, Royce is using the strength of his entire arm against Charles's thumb only.

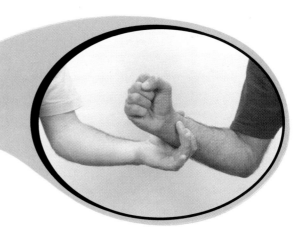

Detail

In this detail we can see that Royce is pulling away from the four fingers and in the direction of the thumb.

3 *Pull your hand away.*

Single-handed wrist grab (thumb down)

In this variation on the escape from the single-handed wrist grab, the aggressor grabs you with his thumb pointing down.

1 Charles grabs Royce's right wrist with his left hand.

2 *Get in base and twist your wrist toward his thumb.* In this case the opening between the thumb and the fingers is to Royce's right. Royce directs the escape toward Charles's thumb, the weakest part of the grip.

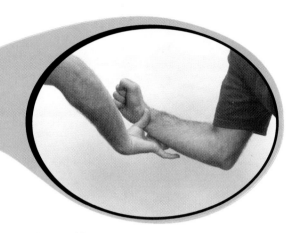

Detail
Note that the direction Royce drives his wrist actually causes Charles's arm to twist, making it impossible for him to resist and keep the hold.

3 *Pull your wrist out.*

Two-handed front choke

You see the two-handed front choke a lot in street fights. The aggressor attempts to choke the victim by grabbing the neck with both hands and squeezing it. Obviously, this attack can be very dangerous. Fortunately, it is easily defended. (This escape is relatively harmless to the aggressor; for a more punishing defense, see position 40.)

1 Charles begins to choke Royce. Royce starts the defense by tightening his neck muscles to prevent damage to his larynx.

2 **Step back in base with your right foot and bend forward.** Royce takes a step back with his right foot and lowers his torso. Notice that Royce is using the power of his entire body against Charles's thumbs. Even a very strong attacker will not be able to prevent this.

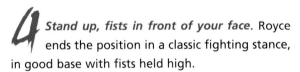

3 *Circle your head around his arm.* Firmly set in base, Royce circles his head around Charles's hands, escaping the choke.

4 *Stand up, fists in front of your face.* Royce ends the position in a classic fighting stance, in good base with fists held high.

Learning to fall backward

Being able to fall correctly is of great importance not only for self-defense but also in day-to-day life. The correct technique can prevent the injuries that often result from the trips and falls common while playing sports or even working around the yard. Here Charles demonstrates the correct way to fall backward.

1 *Put your arms out and check your balance.* Make sure that your torso is centered above your legs and not leaning forward or back.

2 *Squat down.*

3 *Get as low as you can.* If possible try letting your buttocks touch the heels of your feet.

4 *Slowly roll back and hit the ground with both palms of your hands.* Charles breaks the impact of the fall by hitting the ground with his hands first. He also keeps his chin tucked so he doesn't hit his head on the ground at the end of the motion.

Learning to fall to the side

Falling to the side is perhaps the most important of all the falls to learn. It is the proper way to fall from most throws. A great deal of confidence in your ability to handle a street aggression will come when you develop good falling technique.

1 **Step forward with your left foot.** This simple move helps set up the fall.

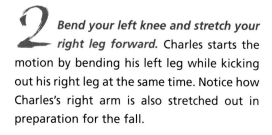

2 **Bend your left knee and stretch your right leg forward.** Charles starts the motion by bending his left leg while kicking out his right leg at the same time. Notice how Charles's right arm is also stretched out in preparation for the fall.

3 *Hit the ground with your butt, not with your back.* It is important to hit the ground with the buttocks and not the back. If your first impact point is your back, you are certain to hit your head on the ground as well.

4 *Help lessen the impact by hitting the ground with your right arm, keeping your head up.* Hitting the ground with a perfectly flat arm will greatly decrease the impact of the fall. Make sure you don't bend your arm when you do this, otherwise your elbow will hit the ground and injury may occur.

Single-handed collar grab

In this classic confrontation position, the aggressor holds the victim by the collar with a closed fist. From there he can punch the victim's face while maintaining full control of the upper body. A similar grip can be used as a choke.

1 Charles grabs Royce's collar with his right hand using a stiff wrist.

2 *Grab his wrist with your left hand and secure the grip against your chest.* Royce uses his left hand to grab Charles's wrist. He holds the grip against his chest to strengthen it.

3 *Step in with your right foot. Right elbow glued to the hip, your right hand strikes his elbow as you step in.* Royce steps forward with his right leg, at the same time using his right hand to hit and lift Charles's left elbow. Notice how Royce's right elbow is braced against his right hip for extra power.

4 *Step around with your left leg and duck under. Control the wrist. The last thing through is the head.* Royce continues the move. He steps through with his left leg and ducks under Charles's right arm while still holding on to Charles's wrist. Notice that the last thing to go through is Royce's head.

5 *Control the arm with both hands. Keep your right hand on his elbow.* Royce is now behind Charles while still holding on to Charles's wrist with his left hand. Royce's right hand holds Charles's right elbow for control.

6 *Lift his wrist to his ear until he submits.* Royce applies a submission hold by lifting Charles's right wrist in the direction of his right ear, creating pressure on Charles's right shoulder. An opponent must yield or suffer shoulder damage.

Forward roll

Few skills are as useful to learn as the forward roll. In addition to fighting applications, it can be used to avoid injuries should you trip while running or fall from a bicycle or a horse. It is similar to the lateral fall only in the way one ends the position. Start slowly as you learn this maneuver, but as you get better at it, you can practice doing it while walking, running, or even jumping over an obstacle.

1 Step forward with your right leg.

2 Bend your body down. Reach down with your left arm until you touch the ground. This is the easiest way to properly learn the correct motion. As you get more proficient, you don't need to literally touch the ground with your hand.

3 Reach back with your right arm as if you wanted to grab something behind you and through your legs. You can never reach too far when first learning this part of the forward roll. The more you emphasize the reaching motion the easier you will make the roll.

4 *Tuck your head and roll over the side of your back, not the spine.* It is extremely important to roll over the side of your back (which is padded by muscles) and not your spine. By rolling over the muscle you will protect your spine from any damage. Imagine yourself doing this incorrectly and rolling over your spine on a paved street—avoid this at all costs!

5 *Continue the roll and prepare to hit the ground with your left hand.* Make one continuous and smooth motion. As with the other techniques, practice does make perfect.

6 *Finish flat on the ground, left arm and left leg straight and head up.* Again, make sure you deflect the impact by hitting the ground with a straight arm to avoid striking it with your elbow.

Headlock with punches

This is one of the most dreaded situations in a fight. The aggressor has the victim by the head while using the opposite hand to strike his face. Strikes to the face can quickly do serious damage. If the victim doesn't know the proper escape, it will be a long day!

Detail
Note the correct way to secure the arm.

Detail
This variation is great when dealing with stronger opponents, as it offers greater control of the arm.

1 Charles has Royce by the neck with his right arm while using his left hand to punch Royce in the face.

2 **Put your right hand in front of your face. Block the punches! With your left arm reach around and grab his biceps**. Royce's first worry is to protect his face and stop getting hit. Royce uses his right hand to cover his face as he reaches to block Charles's left biceps to stop the punches. At the same time, Royce reaches around the back with his left hand and grabs Charles's left arm.

3 *Grab his right wrist with your right hand, step back with your right foot, and look up at two o'clock.* Royce's right hand grabs Charles's right wrist and secures it to his chest. Royce simultaneously takes a step back, using his entire body against Charles's right arm to release the neck hold. It is very important to keep your head aligned with your body as you take the step; this will give you the leverage for the move to work against a strong opponent.

4 *Move your head clear and keep his wrist connected to your chest.* Royce ducks under Charles's arm while still holding Charles's right wrist close to his chest.

5 *Take a small step forward with your right foot.* This side view shows Royce, after having stepped forward with his right leg, still holding on to Charles's right wrist with his right hand while controlling Charles's left biceps with his left hand. Keeping the wrist attached to your chest is key; even the strongest opponent cannot resist with arm strength alone the power of Royce's entire body. Royce can now easily apply a shoulder lock simply by raising Charles's right wrist upward. (For shoulder-lock instructions, see position 8, step 6.)

Hip throw

The hip throw is a very important throw in street fighting and self-defense. It is used in a variety of situations, as you'll see throughout this book. The hip throw is easy to perform and can be devastating. When used correctly against an aggressor, it is usually a fight ender.

1 With your left hand, hold the attacker's right elbow and lock his hand with your armpit. Royce grabs Charles's right elbow with his left hand while at the same time locking Charles's right hand under his left armpit. Now Charles cannot move away and escape the throw.

2 Step around to his side and hold his hip with your right hand. Be square with the opponent. Royce is careful to stay glued to Charles and in good balance in case Charles tries to move away. By being in good base and controlling the hip, Royce is able to foil Charles's attempts to escape.

3 *Step in with your right foot. Make sure your feet are square between your opponent's feet. Lower your body and stick your hips outside his hips.* It is very important to have your hips outside of your opponent's hips, so as to control his body. If you don't get your hips outside enough, your opponent will slide down your outside leg rather than be thrown down.

4 *Straighten your legs and lower your head toward the ground. Pull his right arm across at the same time.* Make sure you use your legs and not your back to lift and throw your opponent. If done correctly, you should be in total control and in full balance as you have your opponent up in the air. A good way to correct the posture and perfect the position is to simply stop when you have your opponent in the air and check your balance. You should be very comfortable and able to walk with your opponent on your back without losing your balance or struggling.

5 *Let go of everything except his arm as you throw.* Keeping hold of the arm will allow you to control your opponent after he is down.

Choke from behind

You would think that being choked from behind is one of the tougher attacks to defend against. Yet there is a very clever and effective defense against this attack.

1 Royce sneaks up behind Charles and starts to choke him. *Grab his right arm with both hands, keeping your elbows close to your body.* By holding on to Royce's arm with both of his arms, Charles relieves the choking pressure on his neck. Note that you add a lot of leverage by keeping your elbows close to your body.

2 *Drop in base.* Keeping your center of gravity lower than your attacker's is key to making step 3 work.

3 *At the same time straighten out your legs and lower your head to the ground, throwing him right over your head, not over the side.* By straightening his legs and lowering his head, Charles propels Royce over his head.

4 *Keep control of his arm as he falls.* Charles wants to keep in contact with Royce's arm so that he can control him on the ground. Make sure you don't hold the arm too tightly and take away some of the impact of the fall, but rather just maintain contact as the opponent goes down.

Overhead club attack

If you are ever attacked by someone with a club, the recommendation is the same as for any other weapon attack—*get away*. Don't try to be a hero; weapons are just too likely to cause serious or fatal injury. If you can't avoid the situation, this defense is very effective.

1 Step in with your left foot to close the distance and reach toward the club with your left arm. Notice the angle of Royce's arm as he tries to grab Charles's wrist. He has his arm bent around 120°, the better to absorb the force of the strike. Also note Royce's hand is in the form of a hook, with all five fingers together in order to avoid getting his thumb caught by the swing of Charles's arms. Once he blocks the strike, Royce will use that hook to keep Charles's hand in place so he can't pull back and strike again.

2 Grab his wrist with your left hand, then reach around his arm with your right hand and grab the club close to his hand. By grabbing near the hand, Royce maintains control of Charles and the club. (See position 25 for the moves to employ if you should fail to secure a grip on the club.)

3 *Slide your right hand to the end of the club and peel the club away, pulling it toward you.* Once Royce's hand slides to the end of the club, he has the leverage to pull the weapon from Charles's hand. Notice Charles's wrist is still secured by Royce's left hand.

4 *Keep your left hand in front of your face and hold the club.* Now in control of the club, Royce still maintains an alert posture.

Standing up in base

Learning to stand up in base is essential for self-defense. Otherwise, if you are on the ground for whatever reason and an aggressor approaches, the act of getting up puts you in a very vulnerable position for those first precious seconds.

1 Put your right arm back on the floor and your left arm in front of your face. Your left leg is planted with the knee up. Your right leg is cocked on the floor, ready to strike. From this position Royce can strike Charles's left knee with his right leg, as well as protect his face and body from strikes with both his left arm and leg. It is important to have your body weight distributed equally between your right arm and left leg.

2 Raise your body with your right arm and left leg, staying in balance and keeping your eyes on your opponent. Royce begins to raise his body using his right arm and left leg. Notice that his hips can move forward or backward for a strike to Charles's knee at any time.

3 *Step back with your right leg and get in a three-point base, left hand in front of your face.* Royce steps back with his right leg and has a firm base with his body weight distributed between his legs and right hand. From this position he can stop Charles from pushing or pulling him.

4 *Stand up in base and be ready.*

Gun at the waist

Again, the best defense against an attacker with a gun is to avoid him altogether. No Brazilian jiu-jitsu technique works against a speeding bullet. Should the attacker be close and have the gun still in his waistband, however, the odds of disarming him are good.

1 Charles has his gun at his waist and starts to reach for it.

2 **Drop down and step in, right hand grabbing the gun, left hand grabbing his elbow.** Royce's right hand blocks Charles from pulling his hand from his waist while at the same time Royce's left hand helps secure control of the arm. At this point Royce's total attention is focused on controlling the gun.

3 *Keeping control of the gun, take a step to his right. Slide your left arm to control his wrist. Keep his elbow close to you and control his arm.* Control the arm with the weapon at all times! Notice Royce pays particular attention to Charles's hand, so Charles can't swing the gun around and fire at Royce.

4 *Hold his wrist with your left hand and bend it back, using your right hand to peel away the weapon.* Still focused on controlling the gun, Royce uses his left hand to apply a wrist lock on Charles's right hand, while he pulls the gun away with his right hand.

Detail

Notice how Royce grabs the barrel of the gun with his right hand for better leverage.

Guillotine (front choke)

Many a fight has quickly ended in a guillotine, or front choke, because the victim loses consciousness quickly, so it is very important to master this defense. We begin with Charles holding Royce in a guillotine, bending him down, and preparing to knee him in the face.

1 Block the knee with both hands. You can't execute a proper defense while getting kneed in the face, so Royce first protects his face by forming a cup with both hands to block Charles's knee.

2 Step in with your right foot and sit back. Still blocking Charles's knee, Royce steps with his right foot between Charles's legs while starting to sit back.

3 *Keep your arms straight as you sit on the ground.* Royce sits back hard, propelling Charles head-first toward the ground.

4 *Don't throw him over you, make him hit the ground with his head.* Note that Royce does not initiate a summersault for Charles; rather, his objective is to make Charles's face hit the ground.

5 *After he lets go, push him to the side.*

POSITION 017

Headlock on the ground (frame escape)

There are so many variations on the headlock that one could dedicate an entire book to the escapes from the position. It is very important when faced with a situation like this to notice the cues your opponent gives you: the position of his head, legs, and body in relation to you. The escape you need to apply is directly related to these variables. For instance, if his head is close to you and his knee is up, an escape with "hooks" (position 39) becomes necessary. Here, Charles has his head away from Royce, allowing enough space for Royce to use the frame escape.

1 Put your left arm in front of his face, keep your right elbow on the ground, and make a frame with your right hand holding your left wrist. By making this frame Royce can keep Charles or even a much larger opponent from squeezing him, as the aggressor cannot get the proper leverage.

2 Put your left foot on the ground, scoot your hips away, and throw your left leg over his face. As Royce moves away from Charles, the pressure of the frame against his face forces Charles to fall back, allowing Royce to throw his leg over him.

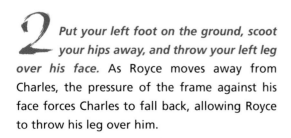

3 *Wrap your legs around his head, cross your feet, and squeeze.* Royce now has Charles's head caught between his legs and applies pressure, causing Charles to release the headlock.

4 *Continue to squeeze until he submits.* Royce doesn't let go of Charles's arm, otherwise Charles would be able to turn to his left, releasing some of the pressure.

Rear bear hug (over the arms)

This is another common situation. The attacker surprises the individual from behind and locks his arms around the unsuspecting victim in a classic bear hug. You frequently see this in multiple-attacker situations, where one aggressor will hold the victim as the others strike.

1 Charles surprises Royce and grabs him from behind, reaching over Royce's arms.

2 *Drop in base.* Royce drops in base (see position 1).

3 *Swing your left leg behind his leg and push your hips close to his leg to knock him off balance.* Royce steps around Charles with his left leg and grabs Charles around the knees. As Royce stepped around, he pushed his hips into Charles's right leg, causing Charles to lose balance. At this point Charles is off-balance and is "sitting" on Royce's left leg.

4 *Lift him with your legs and throw him over your back like a sack of cement!* Royce then uses his legs to lift Charles off the floor and heaves him over his back. Charles will end up on the ground in a very nasty fall.

5 Charles falls to the ground without hitting Royce's leg.

Detail

Make sure you don't bend your knee like this or you will get hurt. In this detail, Royce demonstrates the incorrect way to stand as you throw your opponent. It is very important not to bend your knee while you throw

your opponent. This may cause him to fall on your leg and damage your knee.

Detail

Stand in base, knees square to the ground. In this detail, Royce shows the proper posture for the throw. Note that both his knees are square with the shoulders, as if he were riding a horse. In this manner your opponent will slide down your leg without damaging it.

Two-handed wrist grab

We have already shown two different escapes for the single-handed wrist grab. Another situation that deserves special attention is the two-handed wrist grab. In this case, the assailant uses both hands to grab the wrist and pull the person. As with the other positions, the way to escape is to go in the direction of less resistance—the thumb (as opposed to the direction of the four fingers).

1 Charles uses both hands to grab Royce's right wrist.

2 *Get in base, left hand grabbing under your right hand.* Because Charles is using both hands to grab, Royce counters by cupping his left hand under his right hand.

3 *Use the power of both hands and your body to lift your hand up and out of his grip, working against his thumbs.* Royce now uses his entire torso and his two arms to pry his hand out of the grip. Thumbs alone are not strong enough to resist this.

Front kick

The front kick is an extremely powerful strike. If not properly defended the front kick will cause great harm and may knock the victim down or even out.

1 Charles and Royce face each other. Royce is relaxed and alert while Charles is setting up his move.

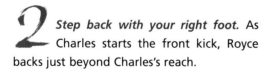

2 **Step back with your right foot.** As Charles starts the front kick, Royce backs just beyond Charles's reach.

3 *Grab his foot with both hands.* Because Royce is just beyond the reach of Charles, he can easily catch Charles's foot at the end of the kick.

Detail

Notice the cradlelike grip Royce uses to catch Charles's foot. Besides being stronger than the regular grip, the cradle will allow a quicker transition for pushing the leg (step 4).

Detail

Royce changes his grip from the cradle before he lifts and pushes Charles. Royce cups Charles's Achilles' tendon with his left hand while his right hand grabs the heel with his fingers pointing up. This allows for much more pushing force than would the cradle grip.

4 *Lift his leg and push him back.* Lifting and pushing Charles's foot will cause him to fall backward.

Side headlock

Attackers love to get their victims in side headlocks because of the control it affords them. Fortunately, this attack can be easily countered with the right technique. Note, however, that a different technique is required if the aggressor is striking you in the face while holding you in the headlock (see position 10). This position begins with Charles holding Royce in a side headlock.

1 *Drop in base with your left forearm blocking his face.* By dropping in base Royce keeps from being pulled down. He holds his posture with a straight line between his head and groin and uses his left forearm on Charles's neck to keep him at a distance.

2 *Squat down and put your right hand under his right knee.* Royce keeps his left hand on Charles's chin and lowers himself, while using his right hand to grab under Charles's right leg.

3 *Lift him by using your hips and legs, not your back.* It is very important to make sure you lift your opponent with your hips and legs, not your back, to avoid any back injury.

4 *Smash him down, making sure you tuck in your head.* Royce drops Charles onto the ground. Because Charles is still holding him in a headlock, Royce tucks in his chin to take away the strain of Charles pulling on Royce's neck as he drops.

POSITION 022

Overhead knife attack

While a skilled knife specialist wouldn't use the weapon in this manner, on the streets you are more likely to encounter this sloppy version. Charles attacks Royce with an overhead motion, knife in his right hand.

1 Step in with your left foot, reach for his wrist with your left hand, and hook his arm. In order to have leverage to block the strike, Royce has his arm at an angle beyond 90°. If Royce's arm was at only 90°, the force of the strike might cause his arm to give enough that the knife would reach his body. Royce makes sure he reaches for Charles's wrist with his hand forming a claw, not a regular grip, to avoid breaking his thumb. Also, once he blocks the strike, Royce wants to keep Charles from pulling back the knife and striking again.

2 *Now reach around with your right hand and hold the wrist. Keep his elbow against your chest for control.* Royce reaches under Charles's elbow and grabs Charles's wrist with his right hand also. By keeping Charles's elbow against his chest Royce assures that Charles won't pull back with the knife.

3 *Keeping control of the wrist and keeping his elbow glued to your chest, bend forward and pull his arm down.* This applies a tremendous amount of torque to Charles's elbow, and he has to let go of the knife.

Front bear hug (over the arms)

There are many dangers from the front bear hug, including pressure on your spine or chest. The attacker can also bend you at the waist and end up mounted on top of you on the ground. If your arms are free to defend yourself, there is a simple defense (position 35), but if the attacker has his arms over yours you have to get a little more crafty.

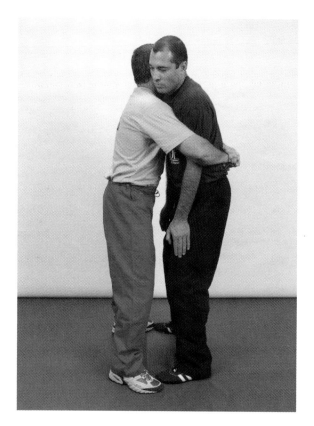

1 Charles has Royce in a front bear hug over the arms.

2 **Put both hands on his hips and drop back in base.** Having both hands with stiff arms on Charles's hips will open up the space necessary for the escape.

3 *Step around to your right, then reach around with your right hand and grab his right hip. Stay in base.* Royce keeps his hands on Charles's hips for distance and steps around to Charles's left side until his body is perpendicular to Charles's body. Royce then reaches with his right hand and controls Charles's right hip.

4 *Grab his elbow with your left hand and step in with your right foot, hips out.* Royce steps around Charles's legs with his right foot and sets up a hip throw. Note that

Royce's feet are pointing forward and are placed inside of Charles's feet. Royce's hip sticks out to the right of Charles in order to maintain control and not have Charles slide down his leg. Royce's right hand holds Charles's hip as well for total control.

5 *Straighten out your legs, bend forward at the waist (lowering your head toward the ground), and pull his elbow across your body.* Royce executes a textbook hip throw.

Hold up (gun in the stomach)

This is probably the most common of the hold-up situations. The attacker has the gun pointed at the victim's stomach in a classic hold up. *Warning:* do not attempt to engage an attacker with a gun unless there is no alternative.

1 Charles points a gun in his right hand at Royce's stomach.

2 *In one motion, pivot on your feet, strike, and grab his hand with your left hand.* Since Charles has the gun in his right hand, Royce pivots in a clockwise direction, clearing his body out of the way of a possible shot. At the same time Royce uses his left hand to strike and control the hand that holds the gun. There can be no hesitation with this move, or you risk being shot.

3 *Grab the barrel of the gun with your right hand, but don't let go of his wrist with your left hand.* Royce now secures control of the barrel of the gun while still making sure that Charles cannot pull his arm away.

4 *Step around with your left foot. Reach around his elbow with your left hand and grab his wrist again. With your right hand push the barrel of the gun toward him.* Notice that Royce traps Charles's elbow with his arm for total control of the arm with the gun.

5 *Grab his hand with your left hand and apply a wrist lock. Peel the gun away with your right hand.* Royce switches his left-hand grip from Charles's wrist to the hand while Charles's elbow is still trapped. By bending Charles's hand toward his elbow, Royce applies a wrist lock, at the same time using his right hand to pull the gun away from Charles.

Overhead club attack (defender misses grip)

Position 13 shows how to stop an attack with a club by blocking and catching the attacker's wrist. But sometimes in employing that defense you will fail to secure the grip on the wrist and the attacker will try to free his club for another strike. This defense is the best counter to that.

1 Charles attacks with a club in his right hand. Royce steps in, left arm at a 120° angle to block the strike, left hand in a claw position to secure the wrist after the block.

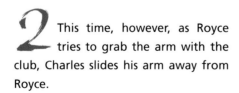

2 This time, however, as Royce tries to grab the arm with the club, Charles slides his arm away from Royce.

3 *Trap his arm under your arm and grab his right elbow with your left hand. Hook your right arm under his arm.* As Charles tries to strike again, Royce traps his arm.

4 *Step around his leg with your right leg. Keep the leg straight.* Royce steps around Charles's right leg with his own right leg and plants the ball of his right foot on the ground just beyond Charles's right foot, blocking him.

5 *Pull his arm across your body and lower your head. Keep control of his arm and throw him.* Royce throws Charles down by lowering his head and pulling Charles's arm across his body.

Headlock (strong opponent)

Position 17 explored escaping from a headlock by using the frame. Sometimes, however, an aggressor will be so strong or tenacious that he won't let go of the hold no matter what. In such cases, a different variation of the escape must be used. In this extreme example, Royce is caught in a headlock, and even though he has used his legs to put Charles's head in a vise, Charles still won't let go. Here is a solution.

1 Royce, while in a headlock, puts Charles's head in a vise with his legs. The stubborn Charles, however, won't let go of the headlock.

2 Let go of everything, scoot your hips away, put your hands on the ground, and go to your knees. Royce starts a different escape, planting his left foot on the ground and using it to scoot his hips in a counter-clockwise direction. He puts both his hands on the ground and goes to all fours.

3 *Clear his legs and mount him, keeping your hands on the ground, and check your base.* Royce uses his right hand on Charles's left leg to push it down, then achieves the advantageous mounted position by passing his right leg over Charles's hips. Additionally, Royce places his left knee near Charles's head and sits on his own heel for better support. Note that in this position it is important to keep the hands on the ground in front of the aggressor so he cannot roll you forward.

4 *Make a frame with your arms on top of his face and lean in with your elbow. Don't try to pull your neck out; let him release the hold because of the pressure on his jaw.* While making sure he still maintains his base by keeping his weight back (sitting on his left heel), Royce places his left forearm on Charles's jawbone and holds his left wrist with his right hand, creating a frame. He shifts his body weight to the frame, applying pressure on Charles's jaw and thus making him release the hold.

5 *Put your left hand on his face, lean forward, pivot your hips, and pass your left leg over his head.*

6 *Hold his arm and lift your hips.* Royce falls back, still holding Charles's arm. By lifting his hips, Royce applies pressure to the elbow joint in a classic arm-bar submission.

Underhand knife attack

More common than the overhead knife attack (position 22) is the underhand knife attack. The aggressor attempts to strike the victim's stomach in an upward thrust. You should practice repeatedly to master this simple yet effective technique so that it becomes automatic.

1 Charles holds a knife in his right hand below or near his waist. Therefore Royce anticipates some type of attack from below.

Detail
Note the proper way to block the knife and grip the elbow.

2 **In one motion, step in with your left leg, block the knife with your left arm, and hook his elbow with your right hand.** As he steps forward with his left leg, Royce uses his left forearm to block the knife and at the same time grabs Charles's right elbow with his right hand, using the claw grip (all five fingers together).

— 72 —

3 Grab his elbow with your right hand and pull him forward. Hook his wrist with your left arm and grab his triceps with your left hand. Royce pulls Charles's right elbow while still blocking his wrist. The pressure on the elbow makes Charles step forward; otherwise he'd break his arm. Royce hooks Charles's right wrist with his left arm and with his left hand he grabs Charles's right triceps to increase control of the knife.

4 Lift your left elbow up and take the knife away. When Royce lifts the elbow, he applies great pressure to Charles's shoulder, making him release the knife.

Single-hand choke against a wall

This is another common aggression in a street fight. The bully holds the victim by the neck and uses his body weight to keep the victim pinned to the wall. From there, he may throw a punch or a knee strike.

1 Charles chokes Royce with his right arm while pinning him against the wall.

2 **Pivot your hips to the right and hit his wrist with your right hand.** Royce hits Charles's wrist with his hand. Since Charles has a lot of his body weight on his arm, he loses his balance and falls forward.

3 *Follow through to the wall with your hand.* Royce continues the arm motion, following through with his elbow, and prepares for an elbow strike.

4 *Strike his face with your elbow.* To finish the move, Royce strikes Charles's face with his elbow.

Gun in the back of the waistband

Position 15 demonstrated how to neutralize an aggressor reaching for a gun in the front of his waistband. Here, however, because Charles is reaching behind his back, Royce cannot simply grab the hand that reaches for the gun; he needs to go for the exposed elbow instead.

1 Charles starts to reach for the gun tucked into the back of his pants.

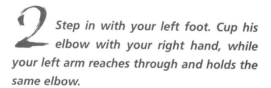

2 Step in with your left foot. Cup his elbow with your right hand, while your left arm reaches through and holds the same elbow.

3 *Pull him forward by the elbow, using your left arm to trap his right arm. Grab his right triceps with your left hand.* Royce pulls Charles's elbow toward him. The pressure from this action on Charles's shoulder makes him step forward. Royce then wraps his left arm around Charles's right arm and his left hand grabs Charles's right triceps, completely dominating that arm.

4 *Lift your elbow up for pressure and take the gun away.* By lifting his elbow, Royce applies a great deal of pressure on Charles's shoulder, making him release the weapon.

Side kick

The side kick is a must in your personal survival arsenal. This versatile strike can be a very powerful blow capable of ending a fight. The target of the kick will vary depending on the situation and personal ability, but it is generally directed toward the stomach area or the knee. Be very careful when practicing this kick against someone else, as you may easily break their knee. It is better to practice the side kick against a dummy or a kicking post.

1 Royce and Charles square off.

2 *Cock your right leg back.* Bend your left leg slightly and don't lean back too much, otherwise you may lose your balance and reduce the power of the kick.

3 *Extend the leg and kick. Kick through your opponent.* For total power and effectiveness, it is important to complete the kicking motion as if you are kicking right through your opponent.

Guillotine counter to a double-leg takedown

The double-leg takedown can be an effective means of taking an opponent to the ground. It can be successfully countered with a guillotine choke. You can sense an aggressor begin to set up for a double-leg takedown because he will take a forward step while lowering his body in preparation for lunging at your knees. To have a successful double-leg takedown, the aggressor will grab behind both your knees while having his waist below your waist. As with all defense techniques, timing is very important, so be alert for these signs to help you time your move.

1 *Step back in base and hook his neck with your right arm.* By stepping back in base Royce adds distance between Charles and himself, making it difficult for Charles to grab his knees. Even if Charles succeeds in grabbing Royce's knees, he won't have the proper leverage to pull Royce's knees to him, because Royce is in effect sprawling by keeping his hips forward and down (the sprawl is a common defense against the double-leg takedown).

2 *Grab your right wrist with your left hand and adjust and tighten the grip around his neck.* Royce's left hand grabs his right wrist and cinches his arm around Charles's neck, making a tight noose around Charles's head.

3 *Pull your right wrist up with your left hand and squeeze.* Royce's left hand pulls up his right wrist and arm, applying pressure to Charles's neck and choking him.

Collar grab with a twisted wrist

In this familiar scenario, a bully grabs you by the shirt and twists his wrist to add pressure and control. The twist is generally used when an aggressor wants to control you by lifting you up, as opposed to using a straight grip to push you back, as shown in position 8.

1 Charles grabs Royce's shirt and twists his wrist.

2 *Grab his hand in both your hands and secure it to your chest. Keep your elbows close to your body and start to twist his wrist.* Royce cradles Charles's hand with both his hands and secures the grip to his chest. By keeping his own elbows close to his body, Royce adds leverage to his hold. He then begins to twist Charles's wrist outward.

3 *Take a step with your right leg, plant the ball of your foot near his foot, and continue to twist his wrist.* By now Charles is completely off-balance and ready to fall. Royce plants his right foot next to Charles's right foot so that Charles can't move to his right to take pressure off his wrist.

4 *Continue to twist the wrist for the takedown.*

Sucker punch

Many times a fight will begin with a sucker punch—an unexpected shot to the face. These come quickly, and there can be little adequate time to defend yourself. If you are in an argument or other situation that you think could turn violent, an excellent idea is to keep your hands high and near your face, just in case. To avoid escalating the situation, you can disguise the real reason you've raised your hands, such as rubbing your hands together as if they were cold or opening them up to make a point.

1 Charles cocks his right hand and begins to throw a punch. Because he sensed danger, Royce already has both his hands high and near his face to have a shorter distance to block any strike.

2 **Step in and block his arms. Put your palms on his biceps, grab his arms, and don't let him pull back.** As Charles takes his swing, Royce steps in and blocks the punch with his left hand. He also blocks Charles's left arm with his right hand to avoid a second strike. Again, Royce uses the hook, or claw, grip to keep Charles from pulling his arms back for another strike.

3 *Hold his right elbow, step around with your right foot, and wrap your right arm around his waist.* Royce maintains control of Charles's right elbow, takes a step around Charles's left leg, and grabs Charles's waist with his right arm. Royce is now in the perfect position to execute a hip throw. At this point it is very important for you to be in base, because your opponent will try to struggle to get away. By staying in base and hanging your weight on him you will easily be able to follow his attempts to escape. There will be a moment in which he stops struggling and regroups for his next attempt at escaping. Wait for that moment to go to step 4. If you try to go to step 4 before you have total control of your opponent, you may lose your balance and fall down with him on top of you.

4 *Step in front of him with your right foot and do a hip throw.* Royce steps in front of Charles with his right foot, makes sure his feet are square and inside of Charles's feet, and executes a hip throw.

POSITION 034

Headlock (bent down)

Position 10 demonstrated an escape from a headlock in which the aggressor is also punching you in the face. In that scenario, you must get in base quickly and stay upright. Here, the aggressor bends you down — seeking to control, rather than punch, you — which allows for this escape variation.

1 Block his knee with your right hand and hug his hips with your left hand. Royce uses his right hand to prevent Charles's left knee from striking him in the face. At the same time he grabs Charles's left hip with his left hand.

2 Step inside his legs with your right leg and begin to sit back. While still blocking the knee, Royce steps between Charles's legs with his right leg and begins to sit down, simultaneously pulling on Charles's hip with his left hand. See position 61 for an alternative scenario in which the aggressor prevents you from coming around the front.

3 *Continue the roll.* The twisting motion of step 2 will send Charles to the ground.

4 *End up mounted on top of him. Put both hands on the ground and check your base.* Royce ends the roll mounted on top of Charles, both hands on the ground for balance. He keeps his left knee close to Charles's head and his right foot on Charles's hip to prevent Charles from escaping.

5 *Make a frame and put your weight on his jaw.* From here Royce can use the frame shown in position 26, step 4 (left hand in front of Charles's jaw, right hand holding his own left wrist) to release the neck hold, or he can simply punch his way out.

Front bear hug under the arms

The front bear hug can be a very uncomfortable situation, especially if the attacker is very strong and starts to apply pressure to the defender's spine. The defense is simple and effective. If the attacker has his arms around yours, however, you must use the defense outlined in position 23.

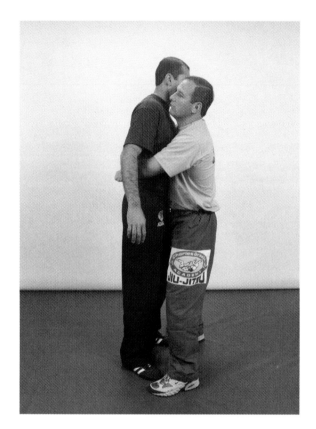

1 Charles holds Royce in a classic bear hug, but Royce's arms are free.

2 **Step back with your right leg and press both palms of your hands against his chin.** Royce takes a step back with his right leg and pushes Charles's chin with the palms of his hands to create space. Charles's neck muscles are no match for the power of Royce's arms, and he must give way.

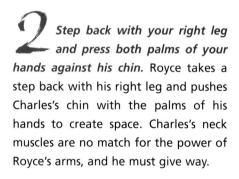

3 *Push his chin up and away.* Royce adds more pressure on Charles's chin and neck by pushing away with both arms. Charles is forced to release the hold.

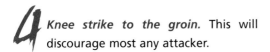

4 *Knee strike to the groin.* This will discourage most any attacker.

Overhead club attack (charge)

This situation is similar to the overhead club attack shown in position 13, except here the aggressor starts his attack from a distance. His swing will have too much momentum to be stopped with the arm catch described in position 13. In this case a small adjustment needs to be made.

1 Charles charges Royce from a distance, swinging a club. Royce is at the ready stance and raises his left arm to protect himself from the strike.

2 **Step in with your left foot and stretch your left arm completely straight. Glue your shoulder to your face.** Since Charles is striking from a distance and has so much momentum, Royce uses his straight arm to deflect the blow and take away its power. By keeping his arm inside the line of attack of the club, Royce deflects the blow. To further protect his head, Royce presses his shoulder tight to his ear, taking away any possible gap for the club to strike his head. It is important to maintain as straight a line as possible between your arm and your torso, so that the club will slide harmlessly down your body. It is equally important to make sure you step inside the club's line of attack, because you do not want the full force of the blow coming down on your arm.

3 *Trap his arm under your armpit and step around with your right leg. Control his body.* Royce traps Charles's striking arm under his arm and steps in for a hip throw, making sure he is in base and in control of Charles.

4 *Step around and do a hip throw.* Royce steps around Charles's left leg, stands in base at Charles's side while still controlling the club arm, and gets set to do a hip throw (position 11).

5 The hip throw.

Choke and drag from behind

This is similar to position 12, but here the strong attacker has managed to start pulling the defender backward. Since you are being dragged back, you can't drop in base and use the escape shown in position 12. This defense will get you out of the situation and put you in a dominant position.

1 Put both hands on his arm, keep your elbows close to your body, and let your body weight hang from his arm. Charles uses both hands to grab onto Royce's choking arm, using the "claw" grip with all five fingers in a hook. He keeps his elbows close to his body for extra leverage and hangs his weight on Royce's arm to relieve the pressure of the choke on his neck.

2 Step around with your right leg and plant your foot behind his right leg. This action stops Royce from continuing to drag Charles. It is important for Charles to keep hanging his weight on Royce's arm to add to the effectiveness of step 3.

Detail

This detail shows Charles's perfect hand position for the throw.

3 *In one motion kick your left leg around and change your grip from his forearm to his biceps.* At this apoint, Charles's feet are in a straight line with Royce's. His right leg is still trapping Royce's right leg. Charles changes the grip of his right hand from Royce's forearm to his biceps in order to stay tight and have more power for the throw.

4 *Bend your body forward, pull his arm across you, and throw him.* Royce cannot help but fall, because his legs are being blocked by Charles's right leg and he cannot step back.

Hold up from behind

Muggers love this technique. They sneak up behind you, stick a gun in your back, and demand your money. This defense works, but, as with all weapons escapes, it is very dangerous and should only be used when you fear for your life and there is no alternative. Here, Charles has a gun touching Royce's back.

1 *Before you start this move, it is important to take a peek back and see which hand has the gun. This will determine which way you escape, as you always want to turn into the gun.* The idea here is to turn into the body of the aggressor so you can apply a bear hug. If the gun is in the attacker's right hand, pivot on your right foot; if the gun is in his left hand, pivot on your left foot.

2 *Here the gun is in his right hand, so in one quick motion pivot on your right leg and bear-hug him over his arms.* Royce makes sure he allows no space for Charles to move and holds Charles's right elbow with his left hand so that he can't pull the gun back and shoot at him.

3 *Trap his right arm with your left arm and step around to his side. Put your right hand on his hip and control him.* Royce adjusts his control over Charles's right arm by trapping it under his armpit. He then steps around, controls Charles's hips with his right hand, and checks his base.

4 *Step in with your right foot and throw him.* Royce steps in with his right foot and does a hip throw.

Headlock (hooks escape)

In this variation of the headlock, Charles prevents Royce from using the frame escape (position 17) by keeping his head close to Royce's. He also avoids being taken backward and down (as will be shown in position 50) by keeping his left knee up and his left foot planted on the ground. However, seeing Charles's left knee up is Royce's cue to use the hooks escape.

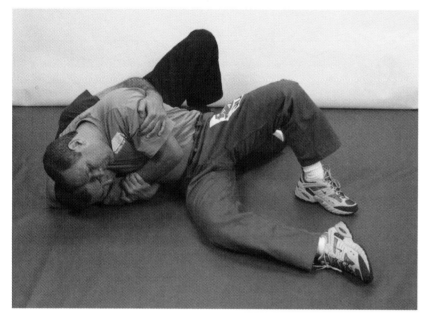

1 Grab his left shoulder with your left hand. Royce grabs Charles's left shoulder and tries to swing his hips away from Charles to bring him down. But Charles anticipates Royce's plan and is able to plant his left leg on the ground to prevent it.

2 Hook his left knee with your left leg, put your right hand on the ground, push forward off your toes, and go to your knees on top of him. Once Royce realizes he cannot bring Charles down, he hooks Charles's left leg with his own left leg. Royce then puts his right hand down and pushes off his right foot and hand to get to his knees and end up on top of Charles, who falls under Royce's pressure.

3 *Let go of everything. Put both hands on the ground and get in base. Keep turning him over.* Royce puts both of his hands on the ground and moves over until he has Charles's left shoulder on the ground. Royce is now in the side-mounted position. Royce keeps both hands on the ground, one in front of Charles's face, so Charles cannot roll him over.

4 *Put your left forearm on his face. Grab your left wrist with your right hand and make a frame. Put pressure on his face by leaning forward on the frame until he lets go.* Royce puts his left forearm on Charles's face and makes a frame by grabbing his own left wrist with his right hand. Royce applies pressure to Charles's jaw by leaning forward into the frame, forcing Charles to let go of the hold. Royce can now apply an arm-bar submission, or punch Charles if necessary.

Front choke (strong aggressor)

We have previously shown in position 5 a very basic and effective way to defend against the two-handed front choke. In that escape, Royce avoided the choke without inflicting any pain on the aggressor. That is useful if you have gotten into a fight with a friend and simply want to protect yourself. In this variation, Royce chooses a more aggressive approach to the escape that ends with a hip throw. This variation works extremely well against stronger opponents. It is also superior in the event that the choke is applied against a wall.

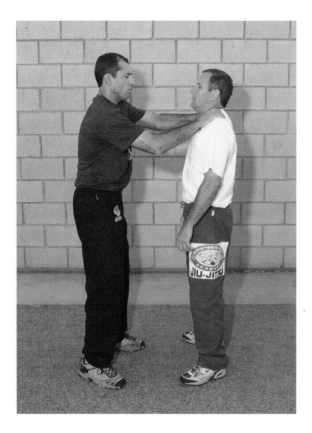

1 Royce attacks Charles with a two-handed front choke.

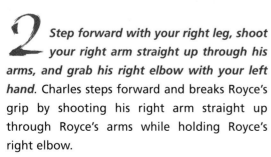

2 **Step forward with your right leg, shoot your right arm straight up through his arms, and grab his right elbow with your left hand.** Charles steps forward and breaks Royce's grip by shooting his right arm straight up through Royce's arms while holding Royce's right elbow.

3 *Pivoting off your right foot, step back with your left leg, both feet pointing forward and inside his feet. Wrap your right arm around his neck and get your hips out for the hip throw.* Charles prepares his body for the hip throw. Pivoting off his right foot, he steps back with his left leg, centering himself in front of Royce and making sure both his feet are pointing forward and are placed just inside of Royce's. Charles exaggerates his hip placement outside of Royce's hips for better control. If Charles's hips are not far enough out, Royce may just slide down as Charles attempts to throw him.

4 *Stretch your legs, head to the ground, and do the hip throw.* Charles executes the hip throw by pushing off his legs to propel Royce's body up. At the same time Charles bends forward, projecting his head to the ground and, with his right hand, pulling Royce's right elbow across his body.

Rear bear hug (under the arms)

A bear hug from behind gives an aggressor great control over your body. He can opt for a simple takedown or can lift you and slam you to the ground. But unskilled assailants will make the mistake of bear-hugging someone while leaving their arms free—allowing for many defense options.

1 Royce has Charles in a bear hug from behind. Notice that this time (unlike in position 18) Charles's arms are free.

2 **Drop in base with both hands on the ground.** Charles drops down in base and places both hands on the ground. This position makes a good four-point base so that Royce can't push Charles forward and smash his face on the ground.

3 *Grab his foot with both hands and pull.* Charles reaches with both hands and grabs Royce's leg behind the ankle. It is important to grab as close to the foot as possible for better leverage. Charles then pulls on Royce's leg as he raises his chest.

4 *Sit on the leg for a knee bar.* Charles sits on Royce's knee joint while still pulling up on his leg, applying tremendous pain to the leg.

Two-handed collar grab (hands apart)

In this position, Charles holds Royce's collar with both hands, controlling his upper body. From here, Charles can easily strike Royce with a knee.

1 Drop in base.

2 Palms together, shoot your hands up through his arms. This will open the space and release the grip.

3 *Wrap your arms around his and clinch your hands.* Royce "grapevines" Charles's arms by tightly wrapping his own arms around Charles's just above the elbows and then clasping his own hands. This grip not only prevents Charles from escaping, but also sets up the throw in step 5.

4 *Step just past his right foot with your right foot and twist your body down.* Royce plants the ball of his right foot beyond Charles's right foot. He keeps his leg as close as possible to Charles's. This will trap Charles's escape route, which is to step around and follow the throwing motion.

5 *Throw him.* Royce throws Charles by twisting his torso while simultaneously pulling Charles's right arm across his body. Note the difference between this and a hip throw. The hip throw uses the hip to control the opponent's body. If you look at a hip throw, you'll see that the opponent is supported by the thrower's hip until he falls down. Here, the opponent is simply tripped by the leg that blocks his leg.

Guillotine (standing up)

Position 16 showed a Guillotine where the attacker bent the victim down. Sometimes, however, an attacker chooses to apply pressure immediately, while the victim is still standing.

1 Put your left hand on his wrist, keeping your elbow close to your body, and hug his back with your right arm. As with any choke, Royce's first concern is to protect his neck. With his left hand he grabs Charles's right hand. Keeping his elbow close to his body increases Royce's leverage. By pulling Charles's arm down Royce relieves the choking pressure. Simultaneously, Royce uses his right arm to hug Charles's shoulder, preventing him from arching up and adding pressure to the choke.

2 Hang your weight on him. Once the choke is loosened, Royce lets his body weight rest on Charles, causing him to further release the choke.

3 Step around with your right leg.

4 *Still holding his wrist, use your right knee to strike his left knee.* Royce knees the back of Charles's right knee, causing it to buckle.

5 *Follow him down, open your left leg, and push your right shoulder into his neck.* Royce stays locked with Charles and follows him down to the ground. It is important to remain tight with your opponent so you don't strain your neck (remember, he is still holding it). Once on the ground, Royce opens his left leg, pushes off his left foot, and presses his right shoulder into Charles's neck. The pressure of Royce's shoulder chokes Charles.

6 *Another option: Grab his right shoulder with your right hand and drive your forearm into his throat.* Royce can also employ a variation of the finish in which he uses the right arm around Charles's back to grab his right shoulder. Now Royce can easily choke Charles by driving his right elbow toward the ground, forcing his forearm into Charles's throat.

Knife attack from behind

In this situation, Charles holds Royce by the neck with his left arm, while holding a knife to his chest with his right. Again, it is never too much to emphasize that quickness and coordination are a must for success in defending any weapon attack. If Royce misses one detail, he may be stabbed.

1 Charles grabs Royce from behind and holds a knife to his chest.

2 *With both hands, cup his knife hand, your right hand outside the knife hand, your left hand inside. Use a stiff arm to keep the knife away and push off your right foot.* Royce drives his left hand into Charles's right hand to keep the knife from stabbing him. At the same time, he uses his right hand to grab the outside of Charles's hand so he can't pull the knife back for another strike. Notice that Royce twists his body away from the knife by pushing off his right foot, gaining distance from the weapon.

3 *Keeping your arm stiff, step back with your right leg and twist his wrist.* As he steps back, Royce puts a wrist lock on Charles by pulling down with his right hand while at the same time pushing up with his left. The pressure will force Charles to release the weapon.

POSITION 045

Two-handed choke against a wall

(bent-finger escape)

In this situation, Charles is using both hands to choke Royce while at the same time pushing him against a wall. Any time a wall comes into play, the constraints of movement make an escape difficult. Here Royce demonstrates a particularly straightforward and ingenious defense.

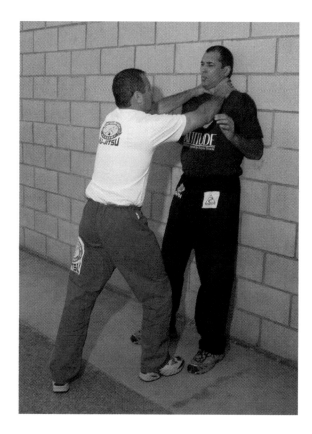

1 Charles is choking Royce against the wall with both hands.

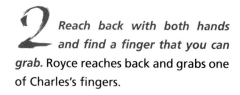

2 *Reach back with both hands and find a finger that you can grab.* Royce reaches back and grabs one of Charles's fingers.

3 *Grab the wrist with your opposite hand and bend the finger back.* As soon as he has a grip on a finger, Royce grabs Charles's right wrist with his right hand to make sure Charles doesn't pull his hand away. He then uses his four fingers to pull Charles's finger toward the back of his hand.

Detail
This detail isolates the way Royce secures Charles's wrist and grabs, in this case, Charles's middle finger with all four of his fingers before pulling it back.

4 This action will break Charles's finger, causing excruciating pain.

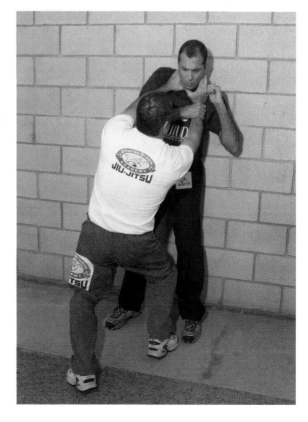

Two-handed collar grab (hands together)

This variation of a collar grab has Charles holding Royce by the collar with his hands together. In this case, the escape shown in position 42 will not work because Royce doesn't have the room to break the hold by reaching between Charles's arms.

1 *Step right, in base, and grab your left wrist with your right hand.* Royce steps right and grips his left wrist with his right hand.

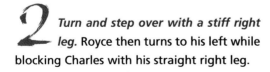

2 *Turn and step over with a stiff right leg.* Royce then turns to his left while blocking Charles with his straight right leg.

3 *Continue to twist and push with your right arm to weaken his grip.* Royce plants his right foot on the ground and continues to twist his body, using that momentum, along with a push from his right hand, to break Charles's grip.

4 *Come back with a reverse elbow strike.* Royce exaggerates the twist and returns with an elbow strike to Charles's face.

Elbow strike

The elbow strike is tough to beat. It can be delivered at very close quarters with tremendous power. It also has the advantage of using one of the pointiest and most resilient parts of the body to strike the opponent. Unlike a punch, which uses the fragile bones of the hand, the elbow strike should be your preferred weapon in any street fight.

1 Keep your hands together near your face. As discussed earlier, it is a good idea any time you sense danger to keep your hands up near your face for protection. Royce does that here, disguising his intentions by rubbing his hands together while talking to Charles.

2 *Twist your body and drive your elbow into his face.* Quickly Royce flicks his left elbow up and drives it toward Charles's face. Royce adds power to the blow by pushing off with his left foot while twisting right.

3 *If possible aim for the jaw.* A solid strike to the jaw will often knock an opponent out.

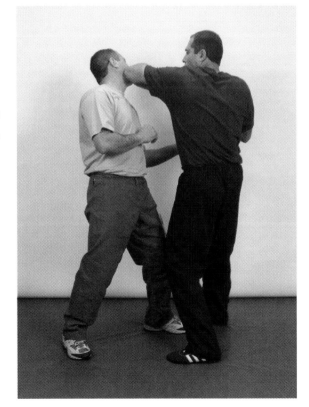

Rear bear hug (lifted up)

In this variation on position 41, Royce lifts Charles off the ground as he bear-hugs him. From this position, Royce could slam Charles on the ground or take him somewhere against his will.

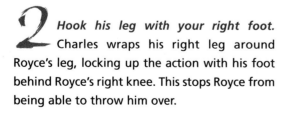

1 Royce has Charles in a bear hug and lifts him off the ground.

2 ***Hook his leg with your right foot.*** Charles wraps his right leg around Royce's leg, locking up the action with his foot behind Royce's right knee. This stops Royce from being able to throw him over.

3 *Bend yourself down and place both hands on the ground.* As soon as Charles blocks Royce's motion, Charles bends his upper body down and places both hands on the ground.

4 *Grab his right heel with both hands and pull, sitting on his knee.* Charles reaches between his own legs and grabs Royce's right foot with both hands and pulls it forward, causing Royce to fall back. Charles finishes the move by sitting on Royce's knee for a knee-bar submission.

Tackle

Though the tackle may seem unsophisticated, it is used by skilled fighters with a wrestling background, as well as unskilled fighters just looking for a way to take the opponent down. In this variation, Royce defends an attempted takedown by Charles and follows with a punishing strike.

1 Charles shoots in for a clinch, perhaps attempting a double- or single-leg takedown.

2 Step back in base with your right leg, both hands on his shoulder. Royce steps back in base with his right leg and uses both his arms to block Charles's shoulder.

3 *Drive your right elbow into his spine.* Royce pivots forward and drops his entire body weight, striking Charles's back with his right elbow. A strike to the spine will cause great pain.

4 (option) *Drive your right knee into his face.* If you have reason to do more severe damage to your opponent, or knock him out, a knee strike to the face will do the trick, as Royce demonstrates here. While still blocking Charles's shoulders, Royce drives his right knee into Charles's face.

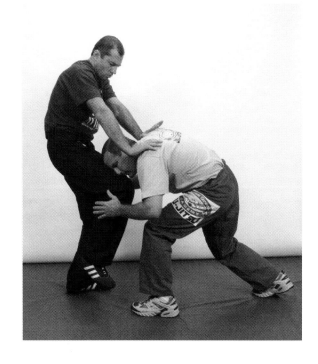

Headlock (kneeling and rolling escape)

Position 17 showed a headlock escape using the frame. In that situation there was enough space between the aggressor's head and the victim to allow use of the frame. In this case, however, Charles's head is so close to Royce's head that Royce cannot make a frame. It is also important to notice that Charles's knees are close together, so Royce cannot make a hook with his left leg between Charles's legs and use the escape shown in position 39.

1 *Grab his left shoulder with your left hand. Scoot your hips away from him.* Royce grabs Charles's shoulder. He then pushes off his left leg to move his hips in a circling motion away from Charles.

2 *Pull him backward and go to your knees.* As Royce continues to scoot his hips away, Charles begins to fall back and Royce facilitates this by pulling Charles's left shoulder toward the ground as Royce goes to his knees.

3 *Let go of everything and put both hands on the ground.* At this point Royce establishes his four-point base with both hands and knees on the ground. It is extremely important for Royce to have his right hand on the ground in front of Charles so he can't roll Royce over his head and end up in the same position all over again.

4 *Clear his knees with your right hand and mount him. Put your left forearm on his face, grab your left wrist with your right hand, and make a frame. Put your weight on the frame. Don't try to pull your head out; make him release the grip because of the pain.* Using his right hand, Royce pushes Charles's knees down and steps over with his right leg to achieve the mounted position. Notice that Royce has his right heel close to Charles's stomach to prevent any possible

escape by Charles. Royce also has his left knee close to Charles's head and is sitting on that heel for tightness and balance. After he has established his position, Royce puts his left forearm on Charles's face (on his jawbone) and makes a frame by grabbing his own left wrist with his right hand. Royce applies pressure on Charles's jaw by leaning forward and putting his weight into the frame, forcing Charles to let go of the hold. From here Royce can step over for an arm bar or simply punch Charles's face to end things. It is also important to remember not to try to pull your neck out, but rather to let the aggressor release the hold due to the pain he feels on his jaw.

Shoulder grab with bent arm

Charles holds Royce's right shoulder by the shirt with his left hand. In this case Charles has a bent arm. From this position Charles could attempt to punch Royce in the face or knee him in the body.

1 *Get in base.* Before he does anything, Royce makes sure he is in base so Charles can't pull him down.

2 *Reach up with your right arm.* To break the grip, Royce reaches up with his right arm inside of Charles's arm, as if he were throwing an uppercut.

3 *On the way down, wrap your arm around his elbow.* On the way back from the motion, Royce wraps Charles's elbow with his right arm. He locks Charles's forearm in position by trapping it with his own armpit. Because Charles had his arm bent, Royce is able to lock the position even more by bringing his own elbow tight against his body.

4 *Grab your right wrist with your left hand. Hips forward, lean back and lift your right arm for the shoulder lock.* Charles no longer can free his arm. Royce grabs his right wrist from below with his left hand and uses it to help lift his right arm up. Royce adds to the submission by thrusting his hips forward as he leans back and lifts his right arm, increasing pressure on Charles's shoulder.

POSITION 052

Shoulder grab with straight arm

In this variation on position 51, Charles grabs Royce's shoulder with a straight arm instead of a bent one. This means Royce will have to finish the defense with a different submission hold.

1 Get in base. Again, before he does anything, Royce makes sure he is in base so Charles can't pull him down.

2 Reach up with your right arm. To break the grip, Royce uses the same technique as in position 51: he reaches up with his right arm inside of Charles's left arm, as if throwing an uppercut.

3 *On the way down, wrap your arm around his elbow. Grab your right wrist with your left hand.* On the way back from the motion, Royce wraps his right arm around Charles's elbow. Royce grabs his right wrist with his left hand and locks his elbow just over Charles's right elbow. Royce locks Charles's forearm in position by trapping it with his own armpit, but in this case, because Charles has a straight arm, Royce cannot bring his own elbow to his body and must go for a different submission.

4 *Step in front with your right leg and twist your body down for the arm lock.* Royce finishes the move by blocking Charles's body with his right leg, preventing any escape. By twisting his body down and to his left, Royce will put pressure on Charles's elbow, breaking it if necessary.

Knife attack from behind

(knife against neck)

This situation is similar to position 44, except Charles places the blade of his knife against Royce's throat instead of his chest. Because this time the blade is close to his neck, Royce cannot simply block it away with his hands, as in position 44, and has to use this defense.

1 Charles has the knife on Royce's neck.

2 **Put both hands on his wrist and drop in base. Keep your elbows close to your body and pull down on his arm.** Royce grabs Charles's wrist with both his hands and drops in base. He pulls down on Charles's wrist to keep the blade away from his neck, making sure to keep his elbows close to his body for extra leverage.

Detail
Note the correct way to grab the wrist. Royce has all five fingers of each hand on the same side and his elbows are close to his body.

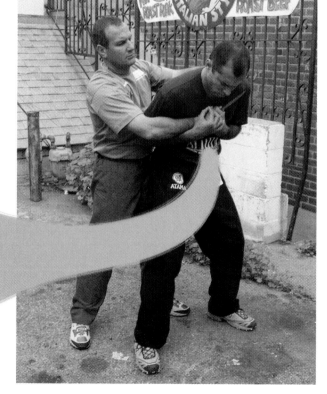

3 *Control the knife. Step around with your left leg.* While making sure he controls Charles's right hand, Royce takes a step back with his left leg and ducks under Charles's right arm.

Detail

Here is a better look at how Royce peels the knife away from Charles's hand by grabbing the handle and pulling it backward. Notice also how Royce is using his right arm to trap Charles's arm.

4 *Pull his arm back. Keep control of his right wrist with your left hand. Wrap your right arm around his right arm and grab the handle of the knife. Pull the handle toward his back and peel the knife away.* Royce continues moving toward Charles's back. At this point Charles is already in pain because, by stepping through and to the back while holding Charles's wrist, Royce twisted Charles's arm. Royce uses his left hand to continue to twist Charles's wrist, applying further pain and forcing Charles to release his grip on the knife. Royce then wraps his right arm around Charles's arm and uses his right hand to easily peel the knife away.

Straight-arm collar grab with high grip

This attack is similar to the single-hand collar grab shown in position 8, but in this case Royce is using a high stiff arm grip on Charles. Charles cannot use the same escape because the stiff arm grip takes away the leverage he would need for the strike to the elbow used in position 8.

1 Royce holds Charles's collar with a straight arm.

2 *Grab his wrist with both hands—left elbow down, right elbow up.* Charles cannot use the escape shown in position 8 because the stiff arm makes it difficult for him to buckle Royce's elbow with a hand strike, as in position 8. Instead, Charles uses both hands to grab Royce's attacking wrist. Notice that Charles is using the conventional grip, with his thumbs on the opposite side of the other four fingers. Charles has his left elbow down and his right one up as he prepares to step across.

3 *Step across with your left leg. Pull his arm with you and over your shoulder. Make sure his elbow is over your shoulder, then pull down on his wrist.* Charles steps around in front of Royce, using a circular motion with his elbows to both break Royce's grip on his collar and pull Royce's arm across and over Charles's shoulder. Charles makes sure that he has Royce's elbow joint positioned on his shoulder and pulls down on the wrist, breaking the arm if necessary.

Pinned against a wall

In this situation an aggressor is pinning the victim against a wall by pushing with both hands. Again, the presence of the wall makes the escape more difficult by limiting the movement options.

1 Charles pushes Royce against the wall.

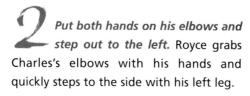

2 **Put both hands on his elbows and step out to the left.** Royce grabs Charles's elbows with his hands and quickly steps to the side with his left leg.

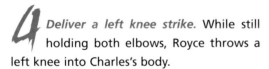

3 *Push him into the wall.* Without Royce's body to hold him up, Charles loses his balance and Royce leads him to the wall.

4 *Deliver a left knee strike.* While still holding both elbows, Royce throws a left knee into Charles's body.

Hand chop

Although Brazilian jiu-jitsu is known for its grappling techniques, rather than its strikes, sometimes the best weapon in a street situation is a quick strike. The hand chop to the neck is powerful and fast, and it may stun an aggressor enough to allow you to escape.

1 Royce is confronted by Charles.

2 **Comb your hair with your right hand.** Royce feigns nervousness, passing his right hand through his hair.

3 *Continue the motion, reaching all the way back.* Royce exaggerates the motion and reaches all the way to the back of his head for greater power on the coming strike.

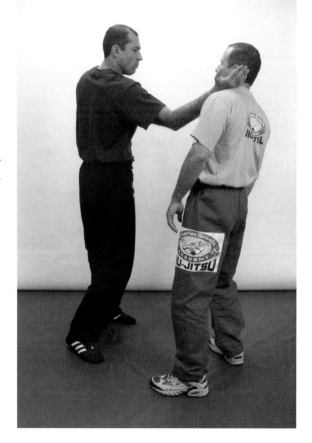

4 *Chop the base of his neck with your right hand, pushing off your left foot and bending your right knee.* Catching Charles by surprise, Royce chops down on Charles's neck with his right hand. Twisting his body to the left, pushing off his left leg, and bending his right knee allow Royce to put his body weight into the strike and generate much more power.

Palm against the chest

Another frequently encountered situation is the hand push. Here, Charles pushes Royce back with a stiff arm against his chest. An elegant and effective defense is shown.

1 Charles has his straight right arm on Royce's chest and is pushing him backward.

2 *Step back with your right leg, secure his hand against your chest with your right hand, and grab his elbow with your left hand.* Royce takes a step back with his right leg and gets in base. With his right hand, Royce secures Charles's hand against his chest, making sure Charles can't pull back. At the same time, Royce uses his left hand to grab Charles's right elbow.

3 *Grab behind his elbow with both hands and bend your body down for a wrist lock.* Royce switches his right hand to Charles's elbow. Now with both of his hands securely bracing the elbow, Royce bends forward, applying pressure to the wrist joint. Charles must submit.

Rear bear hug (over the arms — head butt escape)

In position 18 we saw the traditional defense to a bear hug over the arms from behind, but if you really want to catch your opponent off-guard quickly, a very effective and punishing escape is shown here. For situations where your opponent anticipates the head butt and keeps his head down, see position 59.

1 Royce has Charles in a bear hug, over the arms, from behind.

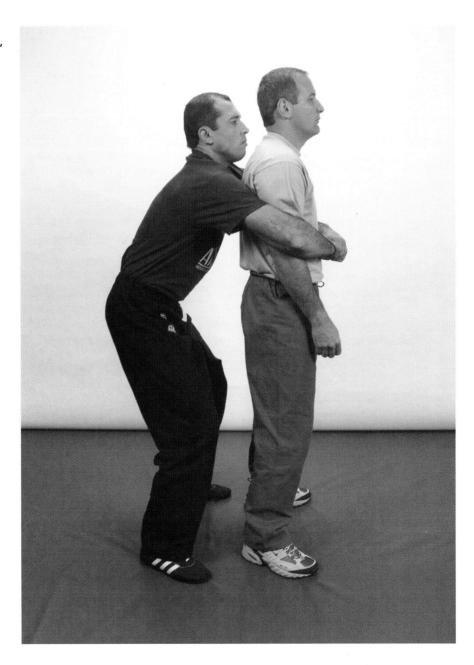

2 ***Drop in base.*** Charles drops in base, knees bent, hips forward, head up, and arms straight out from his body, forcing Royce to bend his knees, which loosens his grip slightly.

3 ***Slam your head back into his face.*** Charles then pushes off with both legs as he thrusts his head back into Royce's face with tremendous force.

Rear bear hug (over the arms — heel strike)

This variation on the bear hug defense isn't quite as devastating as the head-butt defense (position 58), but it can be necessary if the attacker keeps his face tight against your back by dropping in base himself, as Royce does here.

1 Royce has Charles in a bear hug, over the arms, from behind.

2 Charles tries to drop in base but Royce opens his legs and locks his face close to Charles's back, avoiding the head butt.

3 **Strike to the groin.** Since Royce had to open his legs to pull back and keep Charles from falling in base, he leaves himself open for a heel strike to the groin.

Detail
A reverse view of the heel strike to the groin. For successful strikes of all kinds, always picture continuing the strike through the target, not just stopping when contact is made.

Underhand knife attack (straight-arm block)

This variation of the underhand knife attack (position 27) is the better option if the attacker is very powerful. In this case, the defender plays it a little safer, not wanting to take a chance that his block will fail and he will end up getting stabbed. The straight arm used here blocks the stab earlier than the bent arm used in position 27 and doesn't give as easily.

1 Charles has a knife in his right hand and is facing Royce.

2 *Drop in base. Step forward with your left leg. Shoot both arms straight out: your right arm blocks his wrist and your left arm blocks his elbow.* In one motion, Royce drops in base by stepping forward with his left leg and shoots his arms straight out, blocking the stab. Royce's right arm blocks Charles's wrist while his left arm blocks Charles's elbow.

3 *Grab his wrist with your right hand. Step around with your left leg. Pull his arm over your shoulder. Pull his wrist down to break his arm.* Once the stabbing motion is stopped, Royce grabs Charles's right wrist with his right hand. He then steps around in front of Charles with his left leg while pulling forward on Charles's arm until it rests on top of his shoulder. Royce can now break the arm by pulling down on the wrist. Depending on how far Charles's arm is extended over Royce's shoulder, he will either break the elbow or the shoulder joint.

Headlock (bent down — sitting back escape)

In this variation, Charles bends Royce down and, by stepping in front with his right leg, prevents him from coming around the front to initiate the headlock escape executed in position 34.

1 *Grab his left hip with your left hand and put your right hand behind his right knee.* Royce grabs Charles's left hip with his left hand and blocks the back of Charles's knee with his right arm.

2 *Shoot your left leg through his legs and sit back.* Royce shoots his left leg forward between Charles's legs and sits back.

3 *Get on top of him: sit down toward your right heel and clear his right leg with your right hand. Throw your right leg over and mount him.* In a circling motion, Royce sits toward his right heel, simultaneously pulling Charles's hip with his left arm and clearing Charles's right leg with his right hand. Royce continues the motion and throws his right leg over to achieve the mounted position.

4 *Place both hands on the ground. Keep your right heel close to his belly and scoot your left knee close to his head. Keep your base.* Once mounted, Royce adjusts his base. He places both hands on the ground, one on each side of Charles. Royce then moves his right heel to Charles's belly, taking away any space and any chance of escape. He slides his left knee toward Charles's head, shifting his weight to that knee. These are very important adjustments because Royce doesn't want to give Charles the opportunity to roll him over.

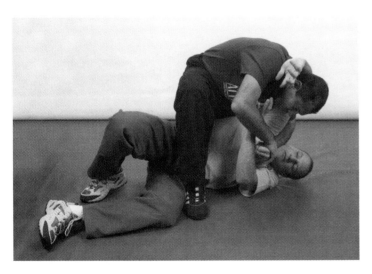

5 *Make a frame: put your left arm on top of his neck and grab your left wrist with your right hand.* To release the neck hold, Royce makes a frame by placing his left arm on top of Charles's neck or jaw, holding his left wrist with his right hand and leaning forward. This applies tremendous pressure to Charles's jaw or neck. Note that Royce does not try to release the hold by pushing with the frame; rather, the frame is used to transfer Royce's body weight to Charles's face and apply pain, which will cause Charles to let go. From this position Royce can go for either an arm lock or a strike to the face.

Underhand knife attack (straight-arm block —

opponent resists)

In this position Charles attacks Royce with a knife from below. Royce attempts the straight-arm defense shown in position 60, but this time Charles tries to pull his arm back as soon as Royce grabs it.

1 Charles holds a knife low in his right hand and attempts to stab Royce.

2 **Drop in base. Step forward with your left leg, both arms straight, and block the stab. Your right hand blocks his wrist and your left hand blocks his elbow.** Royce drops in base by taking a step forward with his left leg and blocks the stab by shooting both arms out. Royce uses his right hand to block Charles's wrist and his left hand to block Charles's elbow. Royce then grabs Charles's wrist with his right hand and attempts to step through, but Charles tries to pull his arm back.

3 *When he tries to pull back, grab his wrist with both hands.* Note that because Royce is in good base he is able to keep Charles from pulling him down.

4 *Step forward around him with your right leg and lift his wrist with both arms.* Royce steps in front of Charles by taking a step forward with his right leg, simultaneously lifting Charles's arm, which he will duck under in step 5.

5 *Step back through with your left leg. Pull his wrist up for a shoulder lock.* Royce continues to move toward Charles's back, stepping around with his left leg and ducking under the knife. He ends up behind Charles, still in control of Charles's right wrist, and twists Charles's wrist for a wrist lock.

Chair attack

In fights that occur indoors an aggressor will sometimes grab a heavy object such as a chair and use it for an attack.

1 Charles lifts a chair over his head and attempts to strike Royce over the head.

2 **Step forward with your left leg and shoot both hands into his elbows.** Royce stops the attack by taking a big step forward with his left leg, stopping the chair early in its motion by blocking Charles's elbows.

3 *Step around to his side with your right leg, right hand holding his right hip.* Royce maintains his left hand on Charles's right elbow. With his right leg Royce steps around to Charles's side. Royce grabs Charles's right hip with his right hand.

4 *Step in front of him with your right leg and do a hip throw.* Once securely in control of Charles, Royce steps around in front of Charles with his right leg and executes a classic hip throw.

Gun from behind (hostage position)

Let us hope you never find yourself in the classic hostage position—being held in front by an aggressor with a gun to your head. Obviously, the severe danger of such a situation requires that you only risk an escape if it seems likely that you will lose your life if you don't do something. There is no room for error here: any action you take must be calculated and precise. In cases like this, it helps to first set up a distraction, enabling you to get in position. A typical distraction is to plead for your life: "Please, think of my wife and kids," you'd say, lightly moving your hands for additional effect.

1 Put your hands up and create a distraction. Royce creates a distraction with dual intent: to get his hands as close to the gun as possible, and to take Charles's focus away from the physical situation.

2 Grab the barrel of the gun with your right hand and pull it away from your face, using your left hand to grab the lower half of his hand. Royce's first concern is to remove the gun from his face. He uses his right hand to grab the barrel of the gun and pull it away from his face in case Charles pulls the trigger. At the same time, Royce uses his left hand to grab the lower part of Charles's right hand. See inset for the proper hand position.

3 *Step around with your right leg. Twist his wrist down with your hands, keeping your arms straight. Don't lose control of the gun barrel.* Royce turns to his right, maintaining total control of the gun barrel, and starts to torque Charles's wrist.

Detail

This is a good shot of the precise grip necessary for best control of the gun. Notice that Royce's right hand grabs the barrel while his left hand grabs the lower part of Charles's right hand, providing maximum leverage to torque the wrist.

4 *Continue to twist the wrist and pull the gun away.*

Single-handed collar grab (thumb down)

In this variation on position 8, Charles grabs Royce's collar with his thumb down. He may have just used that grip from the start or may have reached there by twisting Royce's shirt.

1 Charles grabs Royce's collar with his thumb pointing down.

2 *Step back in base with your right leg and grab his wrist with both hands. Keep your right elbow high, left elbow low.* Royce steps back and grabs Charles's wrist with both hands. Since Royce steps back with his right leg, he has his right elbow up and his left one down. Had Royce decided to do the escape to the other side, stepping back with his left leg, he would have his left elbow up and right one down.

3 *Step around with your left leg and pull his arm under your armpit. Pull his wrist up to break his arm.* Royce steps around to his right and pulls Charles's arm under his left armpit, trapping it. He can then pull Charles's forearm up and break the arm.

Front kick (deflecting the foot)

Position 20 demonstrated a defense against the front kick in which you catch the foot. Both defenses shown in this book are equally effective, but this option may be better when the aggressor is quicker or at a closer distance and you don't have a chance to step back for a good catch.

1 Charles stands in front of Royce, preparing to throw a front kick.

2 **Pivot to the right and swing both arms to deflect the kick.** With no time to step back, Royce pivots his body to the right while using the motion to swing both arms across his body, deflecting the kick.

3 *Put your right hand under his knee, step forward with your left leg, and grab his right shoulder with your left hand.* As Charles's momentum pulls him off balance, Royce grabs Charles under the right knee with his right hand and grabs Charles's right shoulder with his left hand as he takes a small step forward with his right leg.

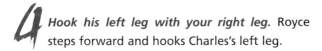

4 *Hook his left leg with your right leg.* Royce steps forward and hooks Charles's left leg.

5 *Kick back with your right leg. Lift his leg with your right hand, pull down his shoulder with your left hand, and throw him.* Royce kicks his right heel back, sweeping Charles's leg. At the same time, he pulls down on Charles's shoulder with his left hand and uses his right hand to push up Charles's leg, causing Charles to fall.

POSITION 067

Knife attack from the side

This variation of the knife attack has the assailant using a sideways stabbing motion.

1 Charles holds the knife in his right hand and prepares to attack Royce. Notice that Royce has his hands up in a "surrender" gesture—this hand position will greatly help his defense.

2 **Step forward with your left foot, then block and hook his wrist with your left hand.** Royce uses the "claw" grip—all five fingers on the same side—to block and hook Charles's wrist. It is important to hook the wrist so that Charles cannot pull his arm back for another stab.

3 *Reach around and grab the top of his hand with your right hand.* Royce uses his right hand to grab Charles's right thumb and hand.

4 *Pull down on his right hand to twist his wrist.* With his right hand, Royce twists Charles's wrist by pulling down on his right thumb, causing Charles to bend down in pain.

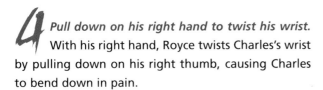

Detail

Note the proper way to control the hand. Royce's right hand grabs Charles's thumb, while his left hooks Charles's wrist with a "claw" grip. This combination is essential to maximize the torque on Charles's wrist.

Collar grab with stiff arm

In this variation, the aggressor holds the victim's collar with a stiff wrist. With any sort of collar grab, the assailant's grip will determine your defense. In this case, the stiff arm presents a problem for Royce: he cannot use the defense shown in position 8 because Charles's stiff arm will make it difficult for Royce to bend the arm with a strike.

1 Charles holds Royce's collar with a stiff arm and wrist.

2
Pivot left, grab his elbow with your left hand, and strike his wrist with your right hand. Royce pivots to his left and uses his left hand to grab Charles's elbow. The pivoting action will cause Charles's wrist to buckle. Royce adds a right-hand strike to Charles's wrist to help make the wrist give. Notice that Royce makes sure he keeps his own elbows close to his body for greater leverage and control. This is especially important when fighting very large or strong individuals.

3
Pull his elbow and bend forward for a wrist lock. Royce secures Charles's right hand against his chest and pulls Charles's elbow toward him as he bends forward, applying pressure to the wrist for a wrist lock.

Detail
Note how Royce keeps his right hand on top of Charles's palm to prevent Charles from pulling his hand out.

Wrestler head-and-arm hold

(bridge-and-roll escape)

The wrestler head-and-arm hold is a very solid control position. The aggressor holds the victim in a headlock while at the same time trapping the victim's arm under his armpit.

1 Charles has Royce in a head-and-arm hold.

2 *Grab your right wrist with your left hand. Cinch your arms against his chest. Plant both feet on the ground and bridge.* It is very important for Royce to bridge straight back over his head, pushing off his feet and lifting his hips as high as possible in one continuous motion. This will put Charles's weight square over Royce's chest, making it easy for Royce to roll Charles over the other side.

3 *Push off with your right leg and roll him over.* Once Charles's weight is correctly distributed over Royce's chest, Royce simply pushes off his right leg and rolls Charles over to the side. From here Royce has a choice of punching his way out or simply applying the frame escape shown in various other headlock escapes, such as position 17.

Backhand knife attack

The backhanded stabbing motion demonstrated here is a bit more uncommon than some of the other knife attacks shown in this book, but it is still an important part of a complete knife-defense repertoire.

1 Charles holds a knife in his right hand, ready to stab Royce.

2 **Step forward with your right leg and drop in base. Make a fist with your right hand and block the knife with your forearm, wrist to wrist.** Stepping forward into base with his right leg, Royce makes a fist and uses his forearm to block Charles's attack.

3 *Grab his wrist with your right hand and push it down. Pull his elbow with your left hand.* Royce grabs Charles's right wrist with his right hand and pushes it down. At the same time, his left arm pulls Charles's elbow back, pivoting around the shoulder. This will work even against a strong aggressor, since Royce is using both arms in perfect leverage against Charles's right arm, pivoting at the shoulder.

4 *Take a big step with your right leg, continuing to push his wrist with your right hand, and pull his elbow down with your left hand.* To continue the submission motion, Royce takes a step with his right leg. His right foot is now firmly planted on the ground so that his leg blocks Charles's right leg, keeping Charles from being able to turn back. Royce continues to pivot Charles's arm around the shoulder joint by pulling the elbow with his left hand while pushing the wrist with his right arm. The pressure on the shoulder will force Charles to release the knife.

Two-handed choke from behind

In a two-handed choke from behind the aggressor has all the advantages: surprise, a superior position, and the chance to quickly incapacitate the victim. The defensive reaction must be swift.

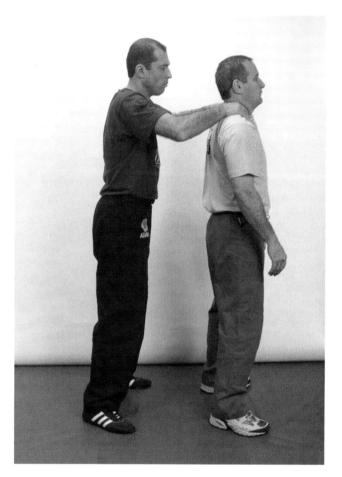

1 Royce slips up from behind and starts to choke Charles with both hands.

2 **With both of your hands grab the top of his hands by the thumbs.** Charles defends the choke by grabbing Royce's hands by the thumbs and pulling them out.

3 *Choose a side. Escape to the left? Then grab the bottom of his right hand with your left hand and step back around with your right leg. Pull his thumb down with your right hand to twist his wrist.* Charles can escape by moving either left or right. Since there is no inherent advantage to either side, you should choose whichever side naturally feels more comfortable to you. Practicing enough that you will instinctively move to the more comfortable side can save you precious seconds in a street fight—just make sure you don't get too predictable, and maintain the ability to move in either direction. In this case, Charles chooses to escape to the left. Pivoting off his left foot, Charles steps back through with his right leg. As he does this, Charles pulls Royce's right hand, twisting it. Charles uses his left hand on the bottom of Royce's to improve his control. Royce starts to fall to the ground because of the pain in his wrist.

4 *Continue to twist the wrist for a submission hold.* Charles continues twisting Royce's hand until he submits. At this point Charles has many options: if he so chooses he can administer severe punishment to Royce by punching, kicking, or even kneeing him.

Haymaker

The haymaker is a favorite of unskilled fighters, who rely on one big punch to finish a fight. This being said, it is very important to master the haymaker defense, as it is a most likely situation to face.

1 Charles starts delivering a haymaker, bringing his fist all the way back and swinging it in a huge arc to generate as much force as possible.

2 *Step forward in base with your left leg and duck. Get in tight with him, both hands behind his knees.* Royce steps forward with his left leg, already in base, and ducks the punch. As Charles's punch goes over the top, his momentum will bring him in to Royce. There is so much energy in the missed punch that Charles practically does a summersault over Royce's back. Royce uses both hands to grab behind Charles's knees.

3 *Lift with your legs, rotate your upper body, and heave him over your back like a sack of cement. Pull him with your left hand and push with your right.* Royce pushes off his legs and heaves Charles over his back, using his arms to aid the rotation by pulling with the left arm and pushing Charles's knee with the right.

4 *Let go of him as he goes over your back.* Again, it is important for Royce to make sure his right leg is as upright as possible, so Charles doesn't hit it and damage the knee as he falls.

Swinging weapon

A baseball bat. A two-by-four. An iron pipe. Many common objects are used as weapons in street fights—usually with the assailant swinging wildly at the victim. This is a very dangerous attack and good timing for the defender is a must.

1 Charles holds a pipe and swings at Royce.

2 **Time the swings and close the gap after the pipe misses.** Royce dodges a couple of swings, timing the attacks. Each time, if necessary, Royce steps back and curves his body backward to let the weapon go by.

3 **Clinch! Lock your arms around his waist. Grab your left wrist with your right hand. Get in good base, with your hips close to him.** Royce lunges forward and clinches right as the pipe misses, making sure he locks his arms around Charles's waist. Royce gets in base, knees bent and hips close to Charles so he can stay with Charles. At this point it is very important for Royce to maintain his base because Charles will struggle to get away from the clinch.

4 *Straighten out your left leg and block his left foot. Sit down toward your right foot.* Royce shoots his left leg straight out, blocking Charles's legs. He then sits back, falling toward his right foot in a rotating motion and pulling Charles with him. This will cause Charles to fall down since his legs are being blocked by Royce's leg and he cannot step back.

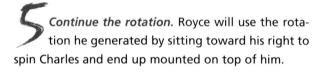

5 *Continue the rotation.* Royce will use the rotation he generated by sitting toward his right to spin Charles and end up mounted on top of him.

6 *End up mounted on him: hands on the ground, left knee close to his head, right knee up.* Royce has his left knee close to Charles's head and has most of his weight on that knee, with his arms on the ground on each side of Charles's head. Royce's right heel is close to Charles's stomach to prevent any escape. He is in perfect control of the situation.

Two-handed front choke

(escape with shoulder lock)

Position 5 demonstrated a basic and effective defense against the two-handed front choke and did not involve any retaliation against the attacker. Here, Royce uses a more aggressive technique that ends with the attacker in a shoulder lock. This is a great option if you need the control necessary to calm down the attacker.

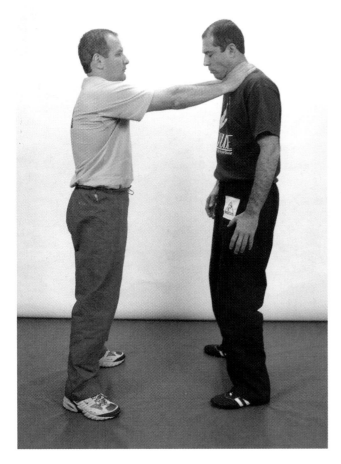

1 Tighten your neck muscles. Royce tightens his neck muscles to keep Charles from damaging his larynx with the choke.

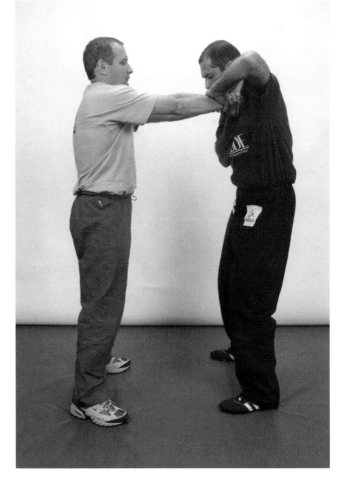

2 Grab his right wrist with both hands: left elbow up, right one down. Royce starts his defense by grabbing Charles's right wrist with both of his hands. Royce has his right elbow down while his left one is up; this will help the escape by adding torque to Charles's wrist.

3 *Step through with your right leg, your foot stepping near his right foot, and duck your head through his hands.* Royce pivots to his left, steps forward around Charles's right side with his right leg, and ducks his head through the gap between Charles's arms and body. Notice that Royce is already adding torque to Charles's wrist by twisting his torso while both hands are wrapped tight on Charles's right wrist.

4 *Keep going to his back, your left leg stepping around to his left.* Royce continues to move to Charles's back, stepping around Charles with his left leg while still in control of the wrist and still twisting it.

Detail
This reverse angle shows the position Royce wants his feet to end in. Notice that Royce has his right elbow close to his body for extra leverage.

5 *Step in with your right foot and push his wrist to his ear.* Royce keeps his elbow tight against his body and steps forward with his right leg, bending Charles's arm into a shoulder lock.

Side kick (defense)

The side kick delivers a lot of force and is often used by skilled combatants. Here, Charles attacks Royce with a side kick to the midsection.

1 Drop in base and lean left. Get your left elbow up, left forearm straight down, and palm facing his foot. Bring up your right forearm to help the block. Since the side kick is a powerful strike, Royce uses both forearms to absorb the impact. Royce also leans to his left to intercept the blow before it reaches full strength.

2 Block the kick and wrap his leg. Put your right hand behind his knee and grab his calf with your left hand. Once he blocks the kick, Royce controls Charles's leg by grabbing it behind the knee with his right hand, while using his left arm to wrap the leg.

3 *Step back around with your left leg, pulling his leg back with you.* Royce takes a step back with his left leg as he pulls Charles's leg with him. Pressing down with his right hand on the knee (put your weight into it) helps force Charles to fall.

4 *Wrap his foot with your left arm and grasp your right wrist with your left hand. Put your right hand on his shin and lean back for a foot lock.* Royce finishes the position by wrapping Charles's foot with his left arm. Royce's left hand grabs his right wrist and his right hand goes on top of Charles's shin. By arching back with his upper body, he applies significant pressure to the foot. Charles must submit. Notice how Royce uses his right knee on Charles's right leg. This serves two purposes: it keeps Charles from getting back up, and it also blocks any heel strikes to Royce's groin or stomach.

POSITION 076

Headlock against the wall

A headlock against the wall is one of the toughest holds to deal with. With the wall limiting your movements and putting pressure on your head as well, this type of headlock ranks high on anyone's list of problem attacks.

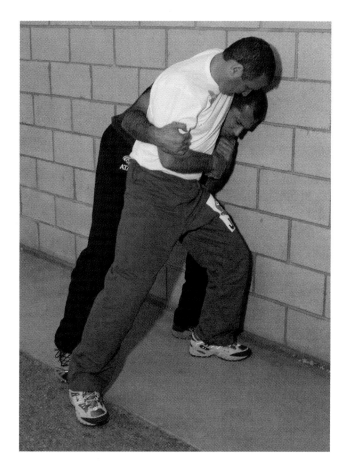

*1 **Grab his left wrist with your left hand and his right biceps with your right hand.*** Royce grabs Charles's wrist and biceps to take the pressure away from the lock.

*2 **Hook his right leg and pull yourself around.*** Royce then uses his right leg as a hook to pull his body around until he is perpendicular to Charles's body. Notice that Royce still maintains his original grips.

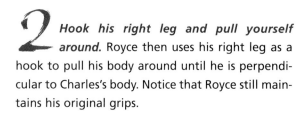

3 *Let go of his biceps and put your right hand on the wall.* At this point Royce releases his right hand and places it on the wall to prevent any attempt by Charles to slam Royce's head against the wall.

4 *Pull his left arm out with your left hand.* From this angle, we can see that the torque inflicted on Charles's shoulder is enough for Royce to easily peel himself out of the hold.

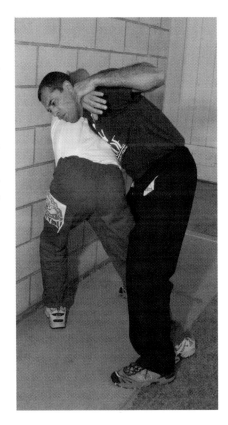

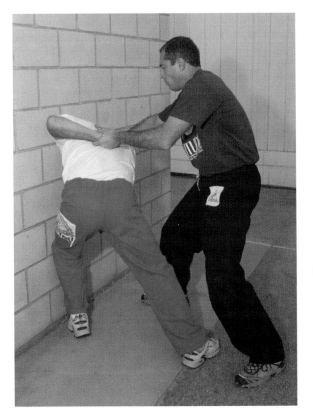

5 *Push his wrist to his ear for a shoulder lock.* Royce applies a shoulder-lock submission by pushing Charles's left hand behind his back and toward his head, applying pressure on the shoulder joint.

Hand slap

This book concentrates on defense, but sometimes the best defense is a little offense. If you want to end a street fight before it has begun, the hand slap to the face can stun an opponent in a flash. Because of its deceptiveness and quickness it is also a demoralizing strike. This is a terrific move for a woman to use when being harassed by a larger man.

1 Talk back to the guy: "Leave me alone. Why are you doing this? I don't want any trouble!" Keep your hands down to emphasize the point. Turn your right shoulder back a little, hands open. Faced with an unavoidable situation, Royce prepares his surprise strike by distracting with words.

2 *Swing your body forward and let your hand go.* The secret of the hand slap is pivoting your body back, then pushing off your rear foot and swinging your body forward very quickly. Just let this motion pull your arm around.

3 *Smack him on the face.* For optimum results aim for the ear. This will make your opponent completely dizzy and give you an opportunity to get away or move in to put him in a submission hold.

Breaking up a fight

Someday you may be forced to break up a fight. This could be a situation where two friends have begun to scuffle or where a stranger has attacked a friend or loved one. One of the many advantages of Brazilian jiu-jitsu is that the grappling techniques it offers allow for complete control of a combatant without necessarily harming him.

1 Charles is beating up Royce's friend.

2 **Put both hands on his shoulders, and push the back of his right knee with your right foot. Bend him back.** Royce grabs Charles by the shoulders with both hands and pushes his right foot into the back of Charles's right leg while pulling Charles back by the shoulders.

3 *Wrap your left arm around his neck.* Royce starts to set up the choke.

4 *Grab your right biceps with your left hand and position your right hand behind his head. Bring your elbows together and choke him.* Once Royce has the proper grip and his left elbow is centered underneath Charles's chin, he can choke Charles by bringing both elbows together, expanding his chest and using his back muscles to squeeze. Squeeze the neck area as if you are hugging an old friend, pressing him to your chest. This pressure will eventually cut off the blood supply to the brain, causing him to pass out. Remember, depending on the situation, you may want to give the aggressor a chance to yield before you make him pass out.

Full nelson

The full nelson is a famously difficult position to escape from. The aggressor hooks both arms under the victim's armpits and grabs behind the neck, completing the lock. If you do get trapped in a full nelson, there are maneuvers you can try (see positions 80, 81, and 82), but the absolute best defense against the full nelson, demonstrated here, is to prevent completion of the lock.

1 Close both arms. Royce anticipates the full nelson and closes both arms to his body, stopping Charles's ability to continue the motion.

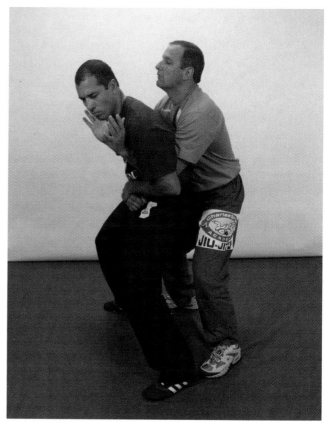

2 Drop down in base. Lock your hands and grab your right wrist with your left hand. Your arms should lock his elbows. After he drops in base, Royce controls Charles by trapping both arms around the elbows.

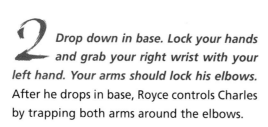

3 *Push off your legs and head-butt him.* Royce delivers a powerful head butt by pushing off his legs and snapping his head back, striking Charles's nose with the back of his head.

4 *Stand straight and deliver a heel strike to his groin.* Sometimes the opponent is very stubborn and won't let go even after the head butt. In such cases a heel strike to the groin will do the trick. Note that steps 3 and 4 can be used in reverse order just as effectively: heel strike to the groin followed by head butt.

Full nelson (can't break out — throw escape)

When you sense a full nelson coming, try to prevent it with the techniques shown in position 79. If you are too late, however, or if your opponent is so strong that you can't stop him from wrapping his arms around you, this move prevents him from completely securing the lock. If you get completely locked in a full nelson, you need to use the escape shown in position 81.

1 Charles surprises Royce from behind, driving his arms under Royce's arms and clasping his hands behind Royce's head and pushing it forward.

2 **Drop in base. Grab your right wrist with your left hand and bring them to your forehead.** Royce drops in base while locking his hands in front of his forehead. In this position Charles can no longer add pressure to the hold.

3 *Step back with your right leg. Plant your right toes past his right foot. Bend forward, head toward the ground, and twist your body to the left for the throw.* Royce steps back with his right leg and plants his right foot past Charles's right foot, blocking his movement. Royce drops down and twists his torso to the left. This will result in a throwing motion as Charles is tripped by Royce's right leg.

4 *He'll land either on his face or his head, with you on top.* Either way the assailant will release the hold.

POSITION 081

Full nelson (completely locked)

In this variation, Charles surprised Royce and was able to lock on the full nelson before Royce could react. The grip is solidly set and Charles has good base, making it difficult for Royce to use any of the previous escapes. This defense is very effective in the event that your opponent in very strong and you are late in reacting to the attack.

1 Charles has Royce in a full nelson, and Royce is unable to break Charles's lock.

2 **Drop in base and lock your hands together, left hand to right wrist, in front of your fore-head.** Royce drops in base and releases the pressure from the full nelson by locking his hands in front of his forehead. No matter how strong the aggressor is, he can no longer apply more pressure with the lock.

3 *Step forward with your right leg and sit back.* Royce stretches his right leg forward and sits down, while pushing off his left leg, forcing Charles to the ground.

4 *As you hit the ground and he releases the grip push back on top of him. Grab his right wrist with your left hand. Wrap your right arm around his elbow and grab your own left wrist. Push his wrist down to break his arm.* Charles releases the hold as he falls down. Royce capitalizes on this pushing off his left leg to get on top of Charles's chest. Royce then grabs Charles's right wrist with his left hand and controls the right arm by wrapping his own right arm around Charles's elbow and holding on to his own left wrist. By pushing down on Charles's wrist Royce can break Charles's elbow joint.

Full nelson (roll and throw escape)

As discussed in position 79, the best defense against a full nelson is to avoid getting locked in one when you feel it coming. Sometimes, however, one does not react quickly enough. This technique works best when the lock is not secured and can still be broken, or if you have more strength than your atttacker and can break the lock. Note, however, that it can still work even if you don't break the lock.

1 Royce has Charles in a full nelson.

2 **Bring both arms down hard to break his grip. Trap his arms under your armpits.** Charles brings both arms down hard, breaking Royce's grip. (This defense will work even if you are unable to break the attacker's grip.) Charles traps Royce's arms under his own armpits. Royce can no longer remove his arms to attempt a punch or escape.

3 *Kneel down on your right knee.*

4 *Roll over your right shoulder.* As Charles rolls over his right shoulder he will throw Royce head-first onto the ground.

Headlock (attacker counters earlier moves)

Here, once again, Charles has Royce in a headlock. This time he has his face close to Royce's, to avoid the frame escape (position 17), and when Royce attempts to pull Charles to the ground (position 50) or hook Charles's legs (position 39), Charles counters successfully each time. But Royce has still another trick up his sleeve.

1 Charles has Royce in a headlock and avoids Royce's first attempt at escaping by following Royce's body as he tries to scoot away from Charles in order to pull him back to the ground (position 50). Notice Royce's right hand gripping Charles's arm to release the pressure from the headlock.

2 *Hook his left leg and try to get on top.* Royce next throws his left leg over Charles's left leg and hooks it. Royce tries to push his body over Charles (position 39), but this time Charles counters by opening his right leg, which prevents Royce from rolling him over.

3 *Spread your legs and push off your right leg, driving your left shoulder into his right shoulder until he lets go.* Royce releases the hook and the shoulder grip and gets to his knees. He spreads his legs and applies pressure to Charles's shoulder by pushing off his toes and pressing his left shoulder into Charles's right shoulder. The pain will force Charles to release the headlock.

Headlock (escape with multiple adjustments)

Street fights are not static situations in which your opponent stands there like a mannequin while you put your move on him. Rather, they are dynamic contests in which your opponent attempts to counter everything you do. This is especially true with headlocks, and it is often necessary for you to go from one escape variation to another as your opponent adjusts to your movements. Particularly against stronger or highly skilled opponents, you may not be able to escape from a headlock by either kneeling and rolling (position 50) or pulling yourself over the top (position 39). Here, Royce faces a very stubborn opponent who won't let go, and he has to add a new escape.

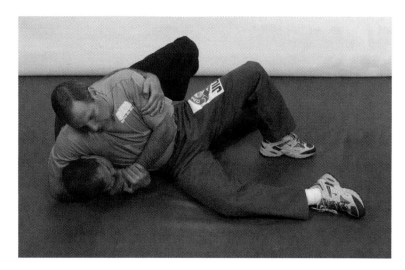

1 Charles has Royce in a headlock with his left knee up. Royce tried to use the kneeling and rolling escape (position 50) but Charles followed Royce as he tried to scoot his hips away. Royce then tries in step 2 to use the escape demonstrated in position 39.

2 Royce hooks Charles's left leg with his own, but, as he attempts to push himself over the top, Charles opens his right leg and resists.

3 *Let go of everything and put both hands on the ground. Go to your knees. Push forward and put pressure on his shoulder.* Royce lets go of everything and goes to his knees. As he pushes forward off his toes, Royce will add tremendous pressure to Charles's shoulder. Many times this is enough for the aggressor to let go of the hold, but Charles is a formidable adversary and he doesn't let go, forcing Royce to go one step further.

4 *Jump to the other side and grab his wrist with your right hand.* Faced with a stubborn aggressor who has a high pain tolerance, Royce continues the motion by jumping over Charles and ending up on his left side. At this point, the pressure on Charles's shoulder is too much and he lets go of the hold. Royce quickly uses his own right hand to grab Charles's right hand and pull it away.

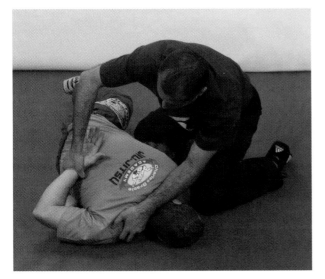

5 *Push his arm to his right ear for a shoulder lock.* Royce finishes the move by using his right hand to push Charles's right wrist toward his right ear for a shoulder-lock submission.

Wall kick

Being trapped against a wall presents special difficulties for defense. Not being able to move away or step back limits your options, and absorbing a blow when you're against a hard surface can be much more damaging.

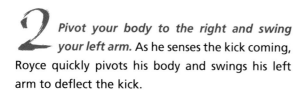

1 Charles has Royce cornered against the wall and gets ready to deliver a right kick.

2 *Pivot your body to the right and swing your left arm.* As he senses the kick coming, Royce quickly pivots his body and swings his left arm to deflect the kick.

3 *Your left arm deflects the kick.* Timing, of course, is a very important factor in this defense, but notice that the arm deflection motion travels a much shorter distance than the kick, thereby giving the defender a safety margin.

4 *Pivot back and strike his face with your right elbow.* As Charles falls forward out of balance, Royce reverses his pivot and delivers a devastating right elbow strike to Charles's face.

Front throat grab

In this situation, Charles grabs Royce's throat with his right hand. From this position Charles can push Royce back or punch him. This defense also works against an aggressor who has grabbed your head by the hair.

1 Charles holds Royce by the neck.

2 *Step back with your right leg and put both hands on his wrist, left elbow up, right elbow down.* Royce steps back with his right leg and grabs Charles's right wrist with both his hands. He keeps his left elbow up and his right one down.

3 *Step in front with your left leg and pull his arm and trap it. Lift his wrist to break the arm.* Royce steps in front of Charles with his left leg and turns while pulling Charles's arm forward. He traps Charles's arm under his armpit and can break it by pulling up on the wrist.

Headlock (bending back)

Here, Royce is not dragging Charles backward by the headlock, as in position 37, but rather just bending him back in a stationary manner. Since he does not have to worry about stopping Royce from dragging him, Charles can just apply this easy escape.

1 *Put both hands on his forearm.* As in any choke, Charles's first move is to protect his neck, so he puts both hands on Royce's forearm and pulls down.

2 *Step around to his back with your left leg. Keep your hips close to his hips.* Charles steps around to Royce's back and pushes his hip into Royce's right hip, his left thigh pushing Royce's right knee and causing it to buckle.

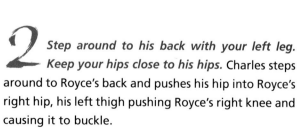

3 *Lift your body and throw him over your back like a sack of potatoes.* Charles will throw Royce over his back by pulling Royce's forearm across his body while twisting his torso.

4 *Hold on to his arm.* Charles keeps a hold of Royce's right arm for control, or in case he wants to administer further punishment.

Gun to the ribs

A gun to the ribs (the side) calls for a slightly different defense than when the gun is stuck in either your front or your back. This position often comes up during car jackings.

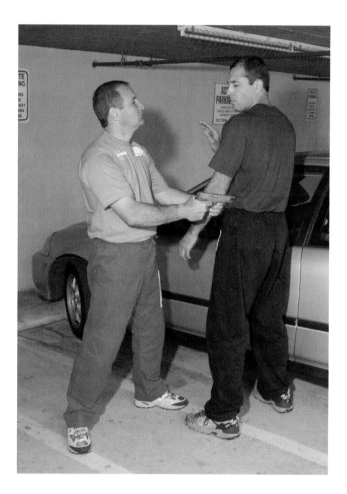

1 Charles sticks his gun in Royce's ribs as Royce prepares to get in his car.

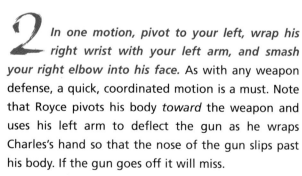

2 *In one motion, pivot to your left, wrap his right wrist with your left arm, and smash your right elbow into his face.* As with any weapon defense, a quick, coordinated motion is a must. Note that Royce pivots his body *toward* the weapon and uses his left arm to deflect the gun as he wraps Charles's hand so that the nose of the gun slips past his body. If the gun goes off it will miss.

3 *Keeping control of his wrist, grab the top of the gun barrel with your right hand and pull it.* It is very important to grab the top of the gun barrel, both for leverage and safety. Royce makes sure he doesn't cover the end of the barrel, in case Charles fires the gun.

4 *Control the gun and keep yourself away from him.* By holding the barrel of the gun, Royce has better leverage and can simply peel the weapon out of Charles's hand. While doing so, Royce maintains a safe distance so that Charles can't surprise him and clinch him to try to take back the gun.

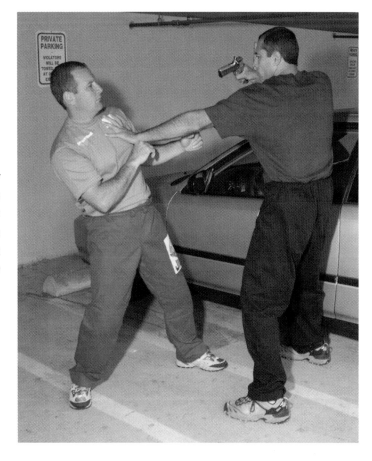

Guillotine choke (pulling up)

Any guillotine choke is formidable, but when well applied by a taller opponent it becomes particularly difficult to defend against. A taller person will be able to lift the victim off the ground, requiring a very specialized defense by the victim. Here, Royce has Charles in a front guillotine and lifts him off the ground as he chokes.

1 *Hug his shoulder with your right arm and put your left hand on his knee.* Charles uses his right arm to hug Royce's shoulder and places his left hand on Royce's leg to help him spring up, easing the pressure from the choke.

2 *Jump up on him, hook the inside of his legs, and grab his wrist with your left hand. Hang your weight on him.* Charles jumps up and hooks Royce's leg; he then switches his left hand from Royce's knee to Royce's right wrist to release the choking pressure on his neck. He hangs his weight on Royce until Royce tires and lets him down.

3 *Step around to his left, putting your left hand back on his knee so he can't knee you, and hit the back of his left knee with your right leg.* As soon as Royce puts Charles down, Charles steps around with his right leg and hits the back of Royce's left knee, buckling it and taking him to the ground.

4 *Put your left knee on his belly and apply pressure to his neck with your right shoulder.* Charles now places his left knee on Royce's stomach and at the same time drives his right shoulder into Royce's neck, choking him.

POSITION 090

Handshake grab

It starts as an innocent handshake between strangers, and suddenly the aggressor won't let go. This can be the prelude to much nastier situations, so it is useful to know how to take charge at this early stage. (For an even faster variation on escaping unwanted handshakes, see position 91.)

1 Charles shakes Royce's right hand and decides not to let go.

2 Drop in base, step forward with your left leg, then reach around his right elbow with your left arm and grab his wrist. Royce now steps with his left leg to Charles's side and wraps his left arm around Charles's right arm until he can hold Charles's wrist. Royce is now in complete control of Charles's arm.

3 *Bend forward and drive his right hand down, grab his right hand with your left, and pull his wrist toward his elbow.* Royce uses his torso to help bend Charles's hand until he can reach it with his own left hand, then applies extreme pressure by bending Charles's hand toward his elbow for a wrist lock.

Detail
Note the correct grip for securing the wrist lock.

4 *Strike his throat with your right hand.* Royce finishes the move by punishing the aggressor with a right-hand strike to the throat.

Handshake grab (quick defense)

If you just want to get out of an unwanted handshake grab and don't need to worry about ending with a submission hold (as in position 90), this is the way to go.

1 Charles and Royce shake hands.

2 Charles won't let go of Royce's hand.

3 *Drop in base, grab your right thumb with your left index finger, and push your knuckle against his hand.* Royce grips his right thumb with his left index finger and drives the knuckle of the index finger between the bones of Charles's hand, directly on a tendon. This is surprisingly painful for the receiver.

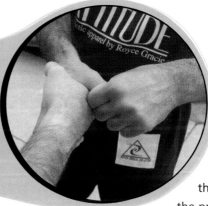

Detail
Here you can see the way the index finger is pushed against the hand. Use the left thumb to apply the pressure.

4 In pain, Charles releases his grip.

Headlock (aggressor against the wall)

Instead of having Royce pressed against the wall, as in position 76, here Charles himself is leaning against it. This situation can arise when the victim attempts to escape and in the scuffle ends up pushing the aggressor against the wall.

1 **Grab his wrist with your right hand.** In this case Royce cannot use his left hand to control Charles's hip because the hip is flush against the wall.

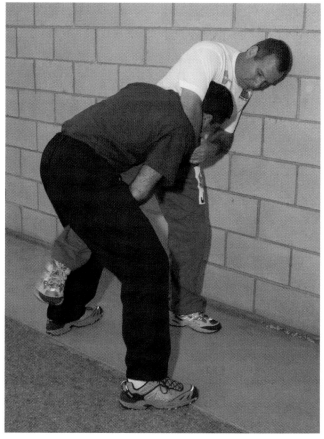

2 **Step around in front. Grab his right leg with both hands.** Royce steps around to his right until he is square with Charles. He then grabs Charles's right leg with both hands and pulls it up off the ground.

3 *Pivoting off your right foot, circle back with your left leg and pull him down.* Royce pivots off his right foot and circles back with his left leg, causing Charles to fall to the ground.

4 *Let go of everything and put both hands on the ground.* Royce's main concern here is to remain in solid base, so he goes into a four-point stance.

5 *Put your left forearm on his jaw and grab your left wrist with your right hand, making a frame. Lean forward and put your weight into the frame.* Royce uses the classic frame to release the headlock. From this angle, we can see that he shifts his weight to the frame, applying pressure on Charles's jaw and thus making him release the hold. Remember not to try to pull your head out of the lock by force; make the other guy submit.

Side-kick defense (aggressor avoids takedown)

In this scenario, as Royce blocks and traps Charles's leg with the technique shown in position 75, Charles avoids the takedown by hopping on his left leg, adjusting to Royce's body position by staying squarely in front of him as Royce attempts a takedown (position 75, step 2).

1 Charles prepares a side kick.

2 **Drop in base and lean left. Get your left elbow up, left forearm straight down, and palm facing his foot. Bring your right forearm up to help the block.** Royce uses the same blocking scheme shown in position 75 (shown here at an earlier stage).

3 **Block and grab the leg, right hand on top, left hand grabbing over the ankle.** Royce is in position for a takedown, but Charles prevents it by hopping on his left leg, forcing Royce to change his strategy

4 *Grab under his knee with your left hand, then switch your right hand and grab his arm.* Royce changes his grip on Charles, his left hand gripping under the knee while his right reaches behind Charles's right triceps.

5 *Hook his left leg with your right leg.* Royce steps forward with his right leg and hooks Charles's left leg, taking away Charles's ability to avoid the takedown in position 75 by hopping and staying squarely in front of Royce.

6 *Lean forward and pull back on his leg.* To execute the throw, Royce leans forward, twisting his body to the left while pulling Charles's right leg back and his right arm across. Charles falls on his back.

Guillotine (arm trapped)

The traditional guillotine choke generally involves surrounding the neck with one arm while grabbing that wrist with the other hand. The choking pressure is applied by pulling up the arm that is wrapped around the neck. We have previously demonstrated two defenses to that situation (positions 16 and 43). In both those cases the defender had both arms free. In this special case, however, Charles also traps Royce's arm in the choke, limiting Royce's ability to defend. Royce no longer has the option of wrapping his arm around Charles's back to keep Charles from arching backward and applying extra pressure on his neck.

1 Charles has Royce in a guillotine choke. Note that Royce's right arm is trapped as well.

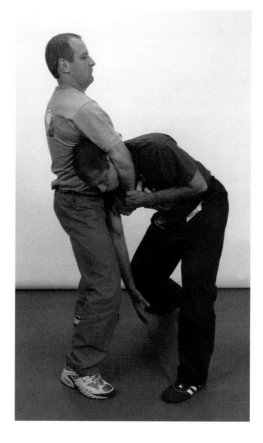

2 *Grab his right wrist with your left hand. Force your right arm down and hang your weight on him.* Royce uses his left hand to grab Charles's right wrist. Notice that after he grabs Charles's wrist, Royce pulls it down by bringing his own elbow to his body to take away the choking pressure. Additionally, Royce pushes his right arm down, hanging his weight on Charles's forearm. Charles has to compensate by bending his knees.

3 *Wrap your hand around his right knee with your right hand. Shoot your right leg forward and sit back.* Because Charles has to bend his knees to maintain his balance, it becomes easy for Royce to reach with his right arm and grab the back of Charles's right knee. Royce then shoots his right leg through and sits back, while still holding Charles's wrist and knee.

4 *Throw him face-first on the ground.* The momentum will cause Charles to be thrown face-first on the ground.

Guillotine (arm trapped — control defense)

This is the same situation as in position 94, but this defense provides you with an option for when you don't want to hurt your opponent, but rather just control him—for example, in the event of an argument with a drunken friend or relative.

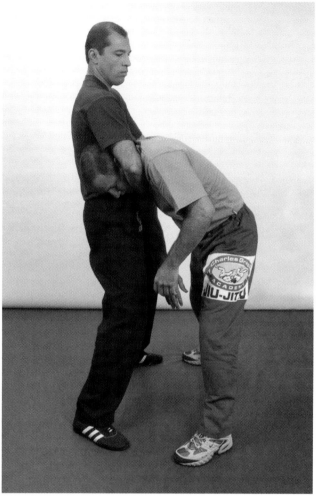

1 Royce applies a guillotine choke to Charles. Charles has his right arm trapped inside.

2 *Grab his wrist with your left hand and pull down. Pivot off your feet and shoot your right arm down and outside his right leg.* Charles immediately uses his left hand on Royce's right wrist and pulls it down to release the choking pressure. Charles then drops down and twists his body to the left, pivoting off his feet, and shoots his right arm through to Royce's right side.

3 *Step forward with your right leg, go around his right leg, and shoot your head back to bust his grip.* Charles steps around Royce's right side with his right leg and straightens his back, shooting his head up as he goes past Royce. This powerful move will break Royce's grip since Charles is using the power of his entire body against Royce's arm. Note that Charles maintains control of Royce's arm.

4 *Step around with your left leg and push his right hand to his right ear for a shoulder lock.* Pivoting off his right foot, Charles steps around with his left leg and positions himself squarely behind Royce. He can now control the amount of pain he delivers, depending on how far he pushes Royce's arm in the direction of his right ear, stressing the shoulder joint.

Choke from behind while sitting down

Not all aggressions begin with words and two combatants facing off. Often the aggressor will use the element of surprise to his advantage and try to catch you in a vulnerable position, such as sitting on a park bench. If the attacker tries to pull you up at the same time that he is choking you, see position 97 for a different defense.

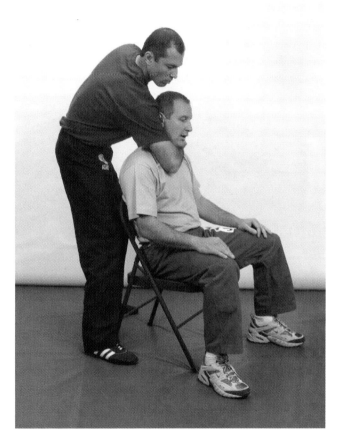

1 Royce gets behind Charles and starts to choke him.

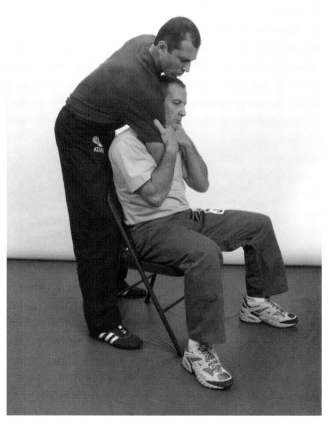

2 **Put your left hand on his forearm and your right on his biceps.** Charles uses his left hand to pull down on Royce's forearm, relieving the pressure of the choke. At the same time he grabs Royce's biceps with his right hand.

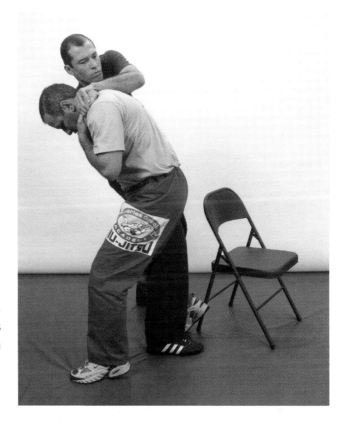

3 *Step back past his foot with your right foot and stand up.* Charles blocks Royce's right leg by planting his right foot just past Royce's right foot. Notice that Charles is using the ball of his right foot on the ground so he can pivot more easily.

4 *Kick around with your left leg.* Pivoting off his right foot, Charles kicks his left leg around, ending up with his body in a straight line with Royce's.

5 *Bend forward to throw him.* Charles bends forward, throwing Royce down. Royce has no option but to fall since his right leg is blocked by Charles's leg.

Choke from behind while sitting down (attacker pulls you up)

Position 96 presented a defense to being choked from behind while sitting down, but sometimes a strong attacker will actually lift you up while choking you, increasing the risk of strangulation and requiring a new defense.

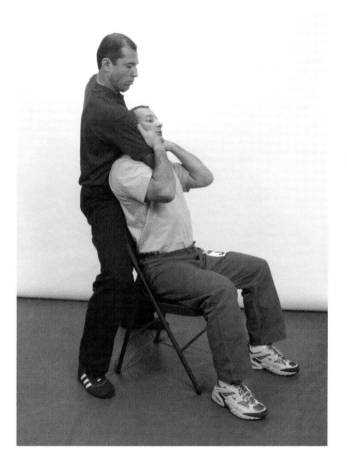

1 Royce sneaks up on Charles and begins to choke him, pulling Charles upward as he does so.

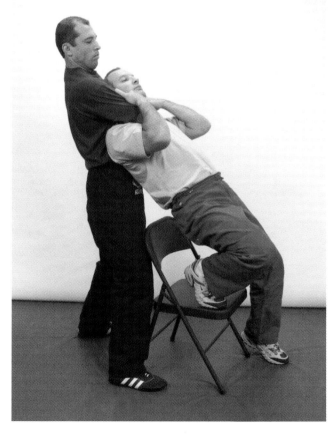

2 **Put both hands on his right arm. Follow the direction of the choke and get up. Put your right foot on the chair.** Your first thought when being choked should always be to defend your neck. Charles uses both his hands on Royce's choking arm to release the pressure. Charles then follows Royce's pulling motion and plants his right foot on the chair (or bench, or whatever you were sitting on).

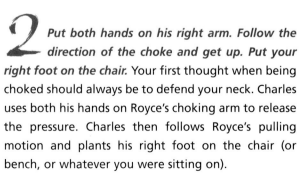

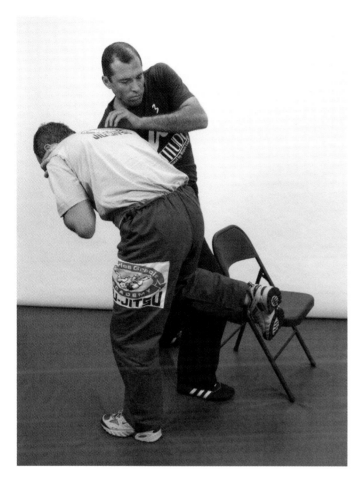

3 *Pivot on your right foot and kick around with your left leg.* Using the right foot as a pivoting point, Charles kicks his left leg to help himself come around. Notice that Charles is still in complete control of Royce's right arm.

4 *When your right foot hits the ground, throw him down by twisting your body.* As soon as Charles is in a straight line with Royce, his right foot is on the ground. Charles throws Royce down by twisting his torso toward the left while pulling Royce's right arm across his body.

Accosted from behind while sitting

You are sitting in a park on the grass, or at a beach, and suddenly a thief sneaks up behind you and tries to grab something and run.

1 As Charles is sitting in the park, Royce sneaks up from behind.

2 Charles is startled by Royce's hand on his shoulder.

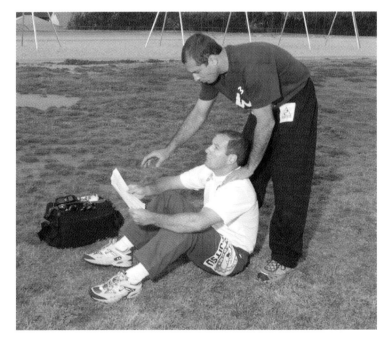

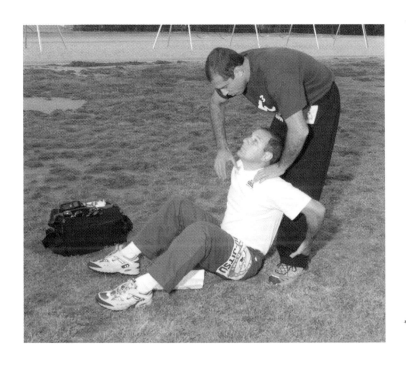

3 *Grab his heels with both hands.* Charles grabs Royce's heels so he can't escape.

4 *Push back with both feet and use your back to throw him down.* Pushing off both feet, Charles drives his body back while still holding on to Royce's heels, knocking him onto the ground.

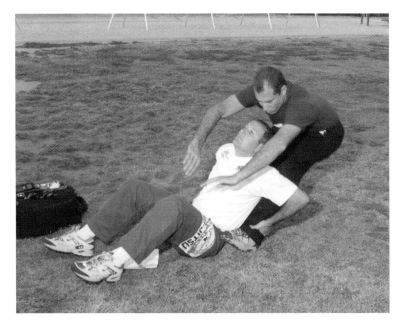

POSITION
099

Side headlock (hip throw)

In this situation, Charles applies a headlock to Royce, but, unlike positions 10 and 34, this time Royce reacts quickly enough that he is able to maintain proper posture with his head up and hips forward, keeping Charles from bending him down.

1 When you feel the headlock, drop in base, bend your knees, head up, hips forward. Grab his right hip with your right hand and his wrist with your left hand. Charles applies a headlock from the side. Royce senses the attack and drops in base to avoid being taken down. At the same time, Royce controls Charles's body by holding Charles's right hip with his right hand and protects his neck by holding Charles's wrist with his left hand. This prevents the choke from being cinched.

2 Step around the front with your right leg. Having secured control of Charles by holding Charles's right wrist with his left hand and controlling Charles's hip with his right hand, Royce steps around in front with his right leg.

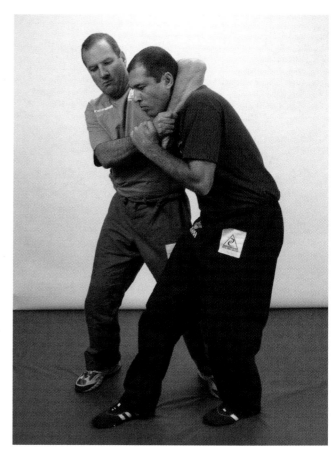

3 *Square your feet inside his feet, hips out.* To properly execute a hip throw, Royce places his hips in front of Charles's hips and squares his feet inside of Charles's feet.

4 *Lift with your legs. Head toward the ground, pull his arm across and do a hip throw.* Royce executes a hip throw, using his legs to propel Charles upward, and dipping his own head toward the ground while pulling Charles's arm across his body.

Arm push

The arm push is extremely common in clubs, where bouncers often try to muscle people back to the street that way. It is also used by kidnappers pushing someone into a car against his will.

1 Royce is pushing Charles by the arm.

2 **Pivot on your left foot and grab his right elbow with your left hand.** Charles quickly pivots on his left foot into Royce and grabs Royce's right elbow so he can't escape. As he does so, Charles also prepares to deliver a left elbow to Royce's face.

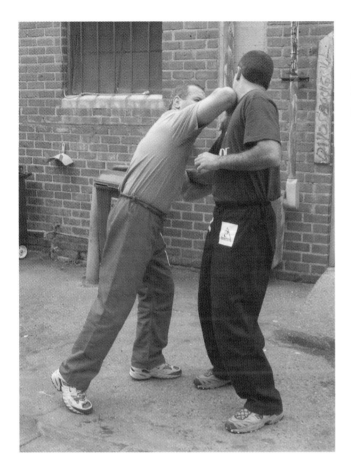

3 *Strike his face with your right elbow and grab his shoulder.* As Charles strikes Royce, he grabs Royce's shoulder and posts his forearm on Royce's neck.

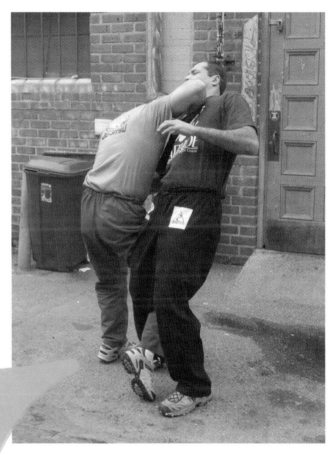

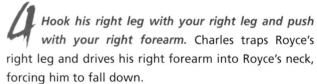

4 *Hook his right leg with your right leg and push with your right forearm.* Charles traps Royce's right leg and drives his right forearm into Royce's neck, forcing him to fall down.

Detail

From this angle you can see the correct placement of the hands and legs for the takedown. Notice that Charles uses his forearm on Royce's throat to drive him back and down.

Half nelson

The half nelson is an extremely effective and widely used control hold. The aggressor reaches around your arm with his arm and grabs your neck with that same hand. It makes for a very uncomfortable position as he applies pressure to the area. The defense shown here is very effective against most opponents, but if the arm grab fails, you can then resort to position 102.

1 Royce has Charles in a half nelson.

2 *Drop in base and trap his right elbow.* Charles drops down in base, head up and hips forward, knees bent. He traps Royce's elbow with his right arm and keeps his right hand close to his chest.

3 *Step around with your left leg. Grab his right wrist with your left hand. Grab your own left biceps with your right hand. Hook his leg with your right leg and pull down on his arm for the submission.* Pivoting off his right foot, Charles steps around with his left leg. Using his left hand to grip Royce's right wrist, Charles locks his right hand to his left biceps, hooks Royce's right leg with his own right leg, and applies a submission hold by pulling Royce's arm down, applying torque to the shoulder.

Half nelson (wrist lock escape)

Position 101 is the standard defense against the half nelson, but strong or skillful opponents will sometimes be able to resist the arm grab shown there. In that case a quick wrist lock will work.

1 Royce gets Charles in a half nelson, trapping Charles's right arm.

2 *Quickly step around to the right with your left foot and trap his right elbow with your right arm.* As soon as he senses the hold, Charles acts quickly and steps away from the pressure, toward his right. At the same time he traps Royce's right elbow under his right arm.

3 *Step behind his leg with your right foot, grab your left biceps with your right hand, then grab his right hand with your left hand and pull it down.* Charles blocks Royce's escape route by planting his right foot just behind Royce's right foot, grabs his own biceps, and applies a wrist lock by pulling Royce's hand down.

Wrestler head-and-arm hold (attacker resists)

A particularly difficult position in a street fight is the wrestler head-and-arm hold, as demonstrated in position 69. In this case, Charles controls Royce's head with his right arm, while at the same time using his left hand to pull Royce's right arm. To make matters worse, Charles pushes off his feet to add his weight to Royce's chest. Royce attempts the bridge-and-roll escape from position 69, but Charles braces with his left leg and arm.

1 Grab your right wrist with your left hand and cinch the hold around his chest.

2 Bridge to the right. When Royce bridges by pushing off his feet and lifting his hips toward the right, Charles stops the motion by bracing with his left leg and arm.

3 *Go to your knees. Grab his right wrist with your right hand, while your left hand controls his back.* Sensing Charles's defense, Royce goes to his knees by pivoting on his left foot and pulling his right leg under and through the space created by the bridging action. It is important for Royce to maintain pressure on his left foot while he pulls his right leg under, otherwise Charles will bring him back to the starting position. Royce controls Charles's wrist with his right hand and Charles's back with his left. The pressure of Royce's left shoulder on Charles's right shoulder, along with Charles's arm being twisted, will allow Royce to easily pull his head out.

4 *Pull your head out and push his wrist to his ear.* This action creates pressure on Charles's right shoulder for a shoulder-lock submission.

The Proving Grounds

Royce Gracie did not step into the Octagon to show that his family's techniques work for him. Royce and the rest of his family have been competing to show that their techniques work for everyone. The mission is to empower people. As Royce puts it, "I step into the ring to prove to everyone, not just other martial artists, that our style works. I want everyone to know that my family's techniques will make them safer. That has been the Gracie mission for over seventy-five years and that is my reason for fighting!"

Pride Grand Prix

Above: Royce with Mark Coleman (left) and Igor Vovchanchin.

Right: Royce in the locker room, concentrating prior to the fight.

Below: Royce addresses the crowd at the Tokyo Dome.

Pride Grand Prix

Above: The Gracie Train goes to Japan. Grandmaster Helio leading the way, followed by Rorion and Royce.

Left: Royce outside the Tokyo Dome, heading for battle.

Below: Grandmaster Helio in the locker room, with sons Royce, Rolker, and Rorion.

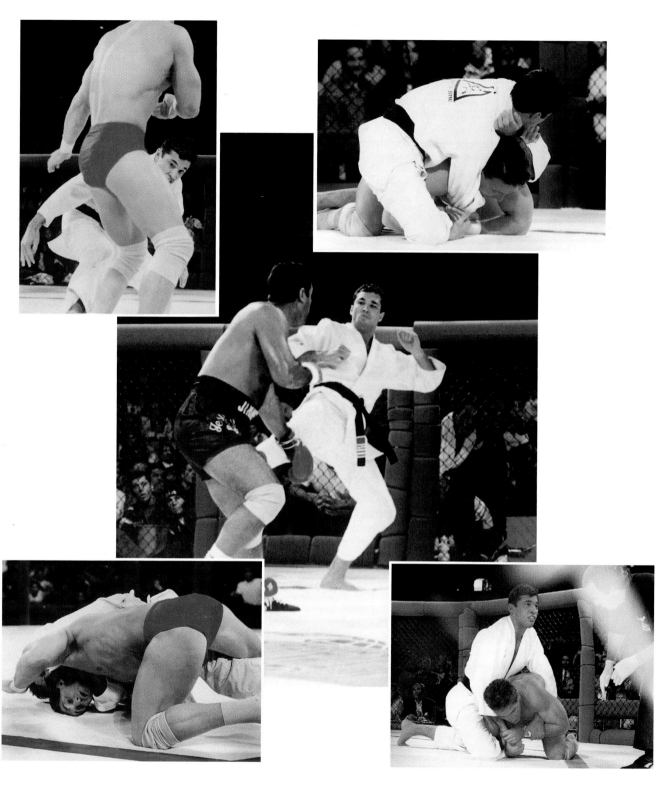

UFC 1

Top left: Royce shoots in on pancrase champion Ken Shamrock in the semifinal. Top right: Royce finishing Shamrock.
Bottom left: Shamrock submits to Royce. Bottom right: Royce speaks to the referee to confirm the submission against Shamrock.
Center: Against Art Jimmerson in the opening match, Royce uses a low kick to set up the lethal clinch.

UFC 1

Above: Royce applying the final choke against European kick-boxing champion Gerard Gordeau in the final match.

Right: Rickson lifts Royce to celebrate the win alongside Royler and Relson.

Below: To the winner go the spoils. After shocking the world with his technique, Royce, surrounded by his family, gets the winner's check (left to right: Helio, Rickson, Royce, Relson, Marianne, Royler, and Rorion).

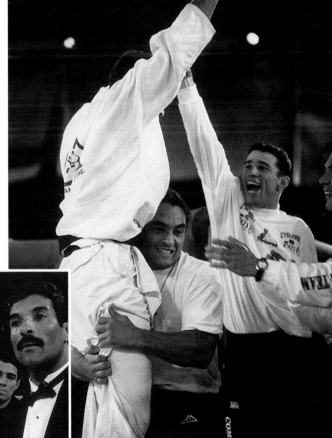

UFC 11

Top left: The famous Royce stare. Listening to last-minute instructions from Rickson. **Top right:** Against European jiu-jitsu champion Remco Pardeol of the Netherlands. Again the low kick precedes the clinch. **Bottom left:** Taking down Japanese fighter Minoki Ichihara. **Bottom right:** The familiar scene—Royce with the winner's check surrounded by family and friends.

UFC IV

Top left: Opening match win over Roy Van Clief. Top right: Final match against Wrestler Dan "The Beast" Severn. Bottom left: Father Helio congratulates his warrior son Royce. Bottom right: Winner's check once again.

California State Championship Superfight

Top left: Charles balancing on top of his opponent. Top right: Charles in control. Bottom: Charles sets up the final choke.

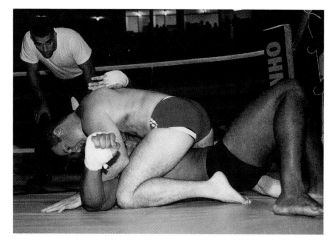

Bahia, Brazil

Top Left: Charles versus Assuerio Silva. With him are uncle Reyson (left) and father Robson.

Top right: Charles mounts Silva.

Left: In full control of the fight, Charles delivers the punishment to Silva.

Below: Charles is victorious against Assuerio Silva.

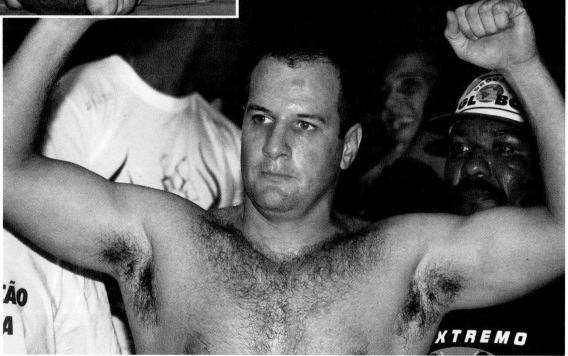

Top left: Royce with Danny Glover and Rorion. Above right: Royce with John Saxon. Bottom: Royce teaching Ed O'Neill from the TV show *Married with Children.*

Royce with a Special Forces student.

Looking at the future: Royce playing with his son Khonry.